CROSS-COUNTRY SKIING IN NORTHERN NEW MEXICO
An Introduction and Trail Guide

by Kay Matthews

Illustrations by Mark Taylor
Maps by Mark Taylor and Barbara Belknap

ACEQUIA MADRE

P·R·E·S·S
Box 6 El Valle Route
Chamisal, New Mexico 87521

Copyright © 1986 by Kay Matthews
All rights reserved, including those to reproduce this book,
or parts thereof, in any form, without permission in writing from
the Publisher

Second Edition, 1993, Revised

ISBN 0-940875-00-4

TABLE OF CONTENTS

	Page
Introduction	1
Ski Touring in New Mexico	3

SECTION I. EQUIPMENT

Skis	7
Skins	12
Poles	12
Boots	14
Bindings	15
Care and Repair of Skis	16
Waxing	18
Clothing	22
Day Pack	25

SECTION II. TECHNIQUE

Basic Cross-Country Stride	31
Uphill Skiing	35
Illustration: Herringbone	37
Downhill	40
Illustration: Snowplow	42
Illustration: Snowplow turn	43
Illustration: Stem christie	45
Illustration: Telemark turn	47
Skating	49

SECTION III. SAFETY

Hypothermia	50
Avalanches	51
Bivouac	51
Frostbite	52
Getting lost	52
Altitude Sickness	52

Physical conditioning	53

SECTION IV. SKIING WITH CHILDREN

Equipment	55
Clothing	55
Planning	56
Lessons	58

SECTION V. SKI TRAILS

Abbreviations	62
Forest Service Offices	63
Map Legend	65

CIBOLA NATIONAL FOREST—SANDIA MOUNTAINS

Cienega Picnic Ground	66
Sulphur Canyon Road	66
Las Huertas Canyon Road	67
Tramway Service Road	67
Kiwanis Meadow Route—Gravel Pit Trail	68
Capulin Trail—Challenge Trail	69
Map: Capulin Trail—Challenge Trail	71
Buried Cable Trail—Switchback Trail	72
South Crest Trail to Tramway	72
Kiwanis Meadow Route—Survey Trail— North Crest Trail	73
Map: Sandia Crest Area	75
10K Trail	76
Challenge Trail	77
North Crest Trail to Tunnel Spring	78

CIBOLA NATIONAL FOREST—MOUNT TAYLOR

La Mosca Canyon Road	79
Map: Mount Taylor Area	'81
San Mateo Canyon Road	82

CIBOLA NATIONAL FOREST—ZUNI MOUNTAINS

McGaffey Lake	83

CIBOLA NATIONAL FOREST—MANZANO MOUNTAINS

Forest Road 55 from Tajuique to Fourth of July
   Campground 83
Red Canyon Campground 84
Map: Manzano Mountains 85
New Canyon—Forest Road 245 86

SANTA FE NATIONAL FOREST—JEMEZ MOUNTAINS

San Antonio Hot Spring 87
Redondo Campground Area
   Redondo Campground 89
   Map: La Cueva Area 90
   Banco Bonito Road 92
East Fork Area
   East Fork Ridge Trail 93
   Mistletoe Canyon Trail 94
   Map: East Fork—Los Griegos Area 95
   Las Conchas Burn Trail 96
Los Griegos Area
   Upper Los Griegos Road 97
   Lower Los Griegos Road 97
   Middle Los Griegos Road 97
   Ladera Trail 98
Peralta Canyon Area
   Corral Canyon Trail—Medio Dia Overlook—
      Calzada Trail 98
   Map: Peralta Canyon Area 99
   Peralta-Peliza Trail 102
   Las Conchas Trail 103
St. Peter's Dome Area
   Del Norte Canyon 103
   St. Peter's Dome, Forest Road 289 103
   Upper Frijoles Ski Trails 103
San Pedro Parks Area
   Bluebird Mesa 105

Vacas Trail	105
Map: San Pedro Parks	106

SANTA FE NATIONAL FOREST—SANGRE DE CRISTO MOUNTAINS

Santa Fe Ski Basin

Black Canyon Campground	108
Pacheco Canyon, Forest Road 102	109
Aspen Vista, Forest Road 150	109
Map: Santa Fe Ski Basin	110
Norski Tracks de Santa Fe	111
Winsor Trail	112

Cowles Area

Irongate Campground	114
Cave Creek Trail	115
Map: Cowles Area	116
Winsor Creek Campground	118
Jack's Creek Campground	118

Las Vegas Area

Carreton Canyon Loop	118
Forest Road 636	119

CARSON NATIONAL FOREST—SANGRE DE CRISTO MOUNTAINS

Taos Ski Valley

Williams Lake Trail	121
Map: Wheeler Peak Area	121
Bull-of-the-Woods	122
Long Canyon—Gold Hill	124

Red River Area

Malette Canyon Road	125
Pioneer Canyon Road	125
Enchanted Forest Cross-Country Ski Area	126
Goose Lake Forest Trail	126

East Fork River Trail	126
Map: Red River Area	127
West Fork River Trail	128
Middle Fork Lake	129

Taos Canyon Area
Mondragon Canyon	130
Garcia Park—Borrego Crossing	130
Map: Taos Canyon	131
Sierra de Don Fernando—South Boundary Trail	132
La Junta Canyon, Forest Road 706	132
La Jara Canyon, Forest Road 5	132

U.S. Hill Area
U.S. Hill—Gallegos Peak	133
Picuris Peak Road	133
Amole Canyon	134
Map: Amole Canyon	135

Peñasco Area
Santa Barbara Campground Road	137
Map: Santa Barbara Campground	139

Tres Ritos Area
Agua Piedra Campground	138
La Junta—Duran Canyon	140
Angostura Canyon Trail	140
Map: Tres Ritos Area	141
Angostura—Agua Piedra	143

Brazos Area
Biscara Trail	144
Maquinita Canyon	144
Map: Maquinita Canyon	145
Map: Brazos Area	147
Little Tusas Creek, Forest Road 133	148
Deer Trail Canyon	148
Forest Road 795	148

  Entrance, Route 5 148
  Burned Mountain, Forest Road 191 148
  Forest Roads 1892, 1893 149
 Valle Vidal Unit
  Powderhouse—Little Costilla Peak Trail 150

CARSON and RIO GRANDE NATIONAL FORESTS—SAN JUAN MOUNTAINS
 Lobo Lodge Road 151
 Chama Community Trail 152
 Map: Cumbres Pass Area 153
 Trujillo Meadow, Forest Road 118 154
 Continental Divide Trail (to Flat Mountain Yurt) 155
 Forest Road 116 (to Neff Mountain Yurt) 156
 Yurt to Yurt Trail 158
 Red Lake Trail, Forest Road 114 158
 Spruce Hole, Forest Road 108 158

Bibliography 159

Glossary 161

Dedicated to all my friends and students who have skied the New Mexico mountain trails with me over the years. Thanks for your company.

INTRODUCTION

Many people spend a lot of time and money "recreating"— playing as hard as they work. Leisure becomes a commodity to fill with activities that test one's physical limits and unburden an overworked and over stimulated intellect. This almost fanatical attention to leisure begins to be characterized as just another job, people striving to find the "best" and "most fulfilling" means of occupying their leisure hours with structured, competitive, and often expensive activity.

What we fail to keep in perspective is our history of what traditionally is meant by leisure. Our ancestors actually spent much more of their day in leisure-time activity, devoting three or four hours a day to work, the rest of the day to visiting, talking, playing games, developing arts and crafts, singing, conducting ceremonial traditions. All these activities, work and play, formed an integrated day, each activity carrying its own importance and significance.

Cross-country skiing originated as an integral part of a day's affairs, a means of transportation. In the northern world communities skis were invented to negotiate necessary travel on snow— hunting, caring for domestic livestock, fighting, trading, etc. As modern civilization invented new, less arduous means of travel, many small communities continued to depend upon skiing to get to work, school, or to other daily activities. Jean-Claude Killy, the famous gold medal Olympic alpine skier, traveled to school on skis in his native France. The love of skiing remained, as the necessity waned, and especially in Scandinavian countries, cross-country skiing became a sophisticated sport with its own special technique and equipment.

Today there is a resurgence of interest in cross-country skiing as people head to the hills to pursue outdoor activity in a physically demanding way. I think this renewed interest bodes well for leisure time becoming a more integrated part of life as well. Cross-country skiing lets you choose your own terrain, who you want to ski with (if anyone), what you want to see and experience, and it's all for free. If you're lucky, you can step out your back door and ski the mountain that sits in your back yard. Otherwise, it's a matter of getting yourself and your skis (and you don't have to spend a fortune to acquire these) into the car and over to the mountain where you can be on your way, free and easy, into the wilderness.

I like to write guidebooks to low-impact sports—sports that require minimal material accouterments and minimally developed support systems. Perhaps I am a purist of sorts, as over the years I've become less fond of driving a car when I can hike, or paying $30 to ride a chairlift when I can cross-country ski for free. But if I am a purist, I think it's for a good reason. Activities that stimulate the human population physically and psychologically, and at the same time encourage and support preservation of our dwindling natural resources, should be promoted over those that require expensive development and exploitation of resources.

I want to see people learn to ski, to get out and enjoy the many New Mexico ski touring areas, but I want them to do so in a consciously caring and responsible way. The two go hand in hand, I think, cross-country skiing and an appreciation of the integrity of our natural world. When you are out there, zooming down the trail on your magical skis, listen to the silence and solitude of the forest and maybe you'll get a taste of what Thoreau meant when he said, "In wildness is the preservation of the world."

SKI TOURING IN NEW MEXICO

Despite its reputation for fairly mild winters, northern New Mexico offers some of the best cross-country skiing conditions available: high mountain trails; miles and miles of backwoods logging roads; warm, sun-filled winter days; spectacular vistas and scenery; hot springs; and good highway access. From Albuquerque north to the Colorado border, from Las Vegas west to Arizona, the Carson, Santa Fe, and Cibola National Forests provide extensive and varied opportunities for ski tours. Many of the trails in the forest system have been marked and categorized as to degree of difficulty by the New Mexico Ski Touring Club and the Forest Service. Standard blue, diamond-shaped blazes on trees designate the trails. Each trail is classified as to degree of difficulty with these symbols:

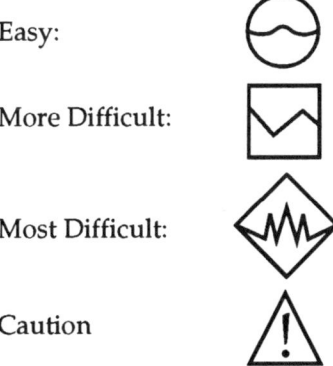

Essentially, cross-country skiing in New Mexico is a combination of two ingredients: sun and snow. In a good snowfall year, depths of snow can reach levels of four and five feet in the higher elevations. Even with averages of only one to two feet, there is usually enough snow to ski from November to April, especially in optimum terrain conditions—northern exposure, tree-sheltered trails providing protection from the sun and prevailing winds. For example, on Forest Road 132 in the Jemez Mountains, the snow can melt quickly or become icy on this open, southern exposed road, while the connecting trail to San Antonio Hot Springs remains snow-covered and pristine in the spruce-fir canopy.

While the sun can ruin the snow quality very fast, it is always a welcome friend on a ski tour, and New Mexico never seems to lack for it. I would always choose a sunny New Mexico day, risking some bare ground or icy patches, over a 0° Minnesota day where the sun is only a fond memory from last August. Ski touring in New Mexico does not have to be a battle with the elements; it's nice to be able to stop periodically and take a scenery break or have a nice, leisurely lunch without turning to ice.

Remember, however, that New Mexico weather can be capricious, and a day which begins with clear skies and bright sunshine can quickly bring blizzard conditions. Always be prepared for any weather contingencies: tire chains, shovel, axe, extra gasoline for your car, adequate food and clothing for you (to be discussed at length in another section). Skiing in a snowstorm has its own special charm and beauty (if you are adequately prepared), and can actually make travel easier, providing excellent snow conditions and invigorating temperatures for the day's adventure.

Ski conditions in New Mexico also vary according to kinds of restrictions in different forests. For quiet, pristine skiing be sure to travel those trails which prohibit snowmobiling. To some skiers there is no greater anathema than the noise of a snowmobile engine reverberating through the forest canyons. Snowmobiles can also be dangerous to skiers on narrow trails with limited views. Some skiers, however, appreciate the fact that snowmobiles can pack down snow that is too deep to ski, functioning like the snowcats which pack the snow at downhill ski areas. I have friends in the Mount Taylor area who try to do most of their skiing mid-week, after the weekend snowmobilers have blazed the trails.

Many excellent ski tours follow Forest Service logging roads. When these roads are unmaintained (unplowed in winter), skiers can enjoy the relatively wide, easy terrain they provide. Unfortunately, when the roads are traveled by four-wheel-drive vehicles or become access to electronic sites, as is the case with the Peralta Canyon Road in the Jemez Mountains, the skiing conditions deteriorate rapidly.

The experienced back-country skier definitely prefers the unbroken trail, untouched by human feet. New Mexico offers many opportunities for this type of skiing, too—high up in the Pecos Wilderness, the meadows above Chama, or even the popular Sandia Mountains near Albuquerque. For the less experienced skier who happens to be the first one out on the trail after a snowstorm, remember to share the trail-breaking duties with the other skiers, or the lead skier will soon tire of plodding along through the snow at a snail's pace while everyone behind glides along in his or her ski track as easy as can be.

There are many available maps of cross-country ski areas in northern New Mexico. National forest maps of all the New Mexico forests are sold at the various ranger district headquarters, supervisors' offices, and the regional office in Albuquerque. These maps provide a good overview of the area, specifically showing the trails, springs, forest roads, rivers, streams and elevations skiers need to be familiar with. Special maps of most of the wilderness areas within the national forests are also available at the appropriate ranger districts and forest headquarters. These maps provide information on topography, trail locations and lengths, wilderness permits (no longer required for entry), wilderness ethics, etc. There is a special cross-country ski map for the Sandia Mountains showing all the marked trails in the area, available at the Sandia Ranger Station in Tijeras Canyon, the Supervisor's Office in Albuquerque, and at various mountaineering stores in the city.

Topography maps, divided into 7.5-minute quadrangles with a scale of 2.6 inches per mile, are published by the U.S. Geological Survey (Denver District Center, Building 41, Denver, Colorado 80225). These maps show the topography of the area with elevation lines indicating canyons, mesas, ridges, valleys, streams, and promontories. While many of the maps are outdated as trail locations and roads change, they still provide the best information for landmarks and elevations.

Maps are included in this book for each ski trip described, indicating locations of trail heads, junctions, and significant landmarks. A bibliography for further reading is located at the end of the book.

The open, rolling terrain of the Jemez Mountains' Valle Grande

Section I. EQUIPMENT

As in many other sports, cross-country equipment becomes more sophisticated, varied, and expensive from day to day. If you think you've just bought state-of-the-art, technologically advanced equipment, just wait until tomorrow and there will be something new available. In this section on skis, boots, bindings, and poles I will present an overview of what is available and also give some guidelines to follow that will help you, as an individual, choose what kind of equipment is best for you.

Remember these words of advice: 1) equipment manufacturers and retail ski stores are in business to make money and will sometimes try to convince you that you must have top-of-the-line equipment to really enjoy and become proficient at cross-country skiing; and 2) the point of cross-country skiing, in my mind, is to avoid the world of matching pink-plastic boots and nylon bunny suits, $30 lift tickets, and $400 ski sets, and still enjoy the snow, sun, sport, and solitude a $100 cross-country ski package can provide.

Skis

TO WAX OR NOT TO WAX?

The first decision you make in choosing a pair of skis is whether to buy waxable or waxless skis. Waxable skis, made of wood or fiberglass, require waxing with a wide variety of waxes to provide both speed and grip. Each kind of wax for each corresponding snow condition provides the proper amount of friction between the ski bottom and snow for downhill glide and uphill climb. I will go into a more lengthy explanation of this in the section on waxing.

Waxless skis, made of synthetic materials, are manufactured to provide grip, or climb, by means of a machine-bottomed pattern—ridges, diamonds, fish scales, etc. These patterns help prevent the ski from slipping backwards when it is pressed into the snow. Unfortunately, this patterned bottom does not work as well for the opposite condition—speed—as does the waxable ski. This actually can be an advantage for speed control, as we're not talking downhill racing here, but fun, safe, ski touring. There are also skis with mohair strips, which work much the same way as the machine-bottomed skis, but as we don't see many of these skis here in New Mexico, I won't go into detail.

I prefer waxable skis. This preference does not necessarily stem from the purist position that waxing is an inherently challenging aspect of the real outdoor person's sport of cross-country skiing (although I won't deny that this is a factor), but comes primarily from a practical point of view: the skier has more adaptability to variable snow conditions with waxable skis. With a wax or klister available to match almost every snow condition imaginable, you definitely feel more in control of the situation. You must learn how to use the wide array of waxes on the market, of course, but if you don't let the whole process intimidate you, waxing can be challenging, fun, and conducive to good-natured camaraderie with your fellow skiers.

I personally love wooden waxable skis because natural materials of any kind appeal to me. I find my wooden skis lovely to behold, and I've easily kept pace skiing alongside those folks on fiberglass skis. Fiberglass skis do have several advantages over wooden ones, though: they are generally faster, and they do not break as easily. Sadly, wooden skis are losing out in the manufacturing game, but if you look long enough you can still find them for sale, and I see no reason for not buying them if you decide that's what you'd like to try. I've had mine for over 10 years, and except for real back-country skiing or the days when that insidious desire for the downhill thrill overwhelms me and I head for the ski slopes with my metal-edged, fiberglass skis, I tour with them on a regular basis.

To help you decide which kind of ski—waxable or waxless—you should buy, consider carefully what kind of skiing you intend to pursue. If you are a beginner, and know that you will probably be a weekend, casual skier for the next few years, invest in a waxless ski and you'll do just fine. Once you've mastered technique and feel comfortable on your skis, you can always invest in a waxable pair. (Take your old ones down to the ski swap and you won't have to spend that much more on a new pair.) By this time you'll probably already know all about waxing from having listened to your friends on waxable skis debate what color wax to use on all your ski trips together. If you keep your old waxless skis, as you become a better skier you can choose from either pair for the type of snow conditions and tour you intend to ski. Before you invest in any skis, try out the different kinds of rentals available, talk to the salespeople at a favorite mountaineering store, and read on for some things to look for when deciding what brand and how much to spend.

CAMBER

All skis, whether waxless or waxable, have a certain amount of "purchase" or "camber." What this refers to is the ski's stiffness or flexibility when it contacts the snow under your weight. When you stand your skis vertically on end, and push them together until there is no air space, this indicates a stiff or soft camber, or how flexible they are for the kind of skiing you intend to do. A soft camber ski is more forgiving, and will bite the snow for better uphill grip. It also turns better in powder or slow-speed skiing. A stiff camber is a faster ski, and requires more weight and control to grip effectively. For the expert or racer it provides better edge control for turns.

According to the experts, the real test for good flexibility is the paper test. Stand on the skis on a hard floor and have a friend slip a piece of paper under the skis where your feet are placed. If the paper slides through easily, the skis have the proper flex and are right for you. If the paper won't slide through at all, the skis are too flexible or soft. If there is too much room between the skis and floor, the skis are too stiff.

SKI LENGTHS AND WIDTHS

Most cross-country skiers measure ski lengths as old time downhillers used to (it's become popular to ski on shorter skis): you should be able to dangle your hand over the tip of the upright ski. If you are particularly light or heavy, you might want to adjust the ski length to take this into account. The lighter you are the shorter the ski you'll choose; the heavier, the longer.

The width of skis depends upon their purpose. Back-country touring skis, at about 55 millimeters wide, are the widest ski and provide the sturdiness you need for more rugged skiing conditions. Light touring skis, at about 48-51 millimeters wide, are lighter and more flexible for shorter trips and easier maneuverability. This is the most popular width and probably what most beginners should choose.

The narrowest ski of the lot, the racing ski, is obviously designed for lightness and speed, and is usually harder to turn than the various touring skis.

WAXLESS SKIS

There are many patterns used on waxless skis, which all work to prevent slipping. The fish scale is probably the most widely used, but companies which don't hold that patent use diamonds, ridges, steps, etc. How tight the pattern is determines how much friction there will be: the tighter it is the better control it has on uphill terrain, but at the expense of speed. The same is true for pattern depth: the deeper the machine work, the more friction.

Manufacturers debate the merits of the "positive base" pattern—that which protrudes from the base—and the "negative base" pattern—that which is incised into the bottom. Generally, the positive base ski provides the better grip. Manufacturers also debate how much of the running surface the pattern should cover. There are many varieties available.

One thing to keep in mind when choosing a machine-bottomed ski is its repairableness. Find out from the store if the ski manufacturer or the store can replace the ski bottom if you wear out the pattern. A word of warning to those of you renting waxless skis: check your ski bottoms for wear before you ever take them out of the shop or you may find yourself struggling for control all day. I once led an intermediate class along a fairly difficult route that became tortuous for one of the students because her rented skis had practically no fish scale pattern left. We ended up waxing them to get her off the mountain.

METAL-EDGED SKIS

These are the high-tech skis of cross-country skiing, the closest thing to downhill skis, providing maneuverability, control, and speed. They are essential for good telemark skiing.

Metal-edged skis come equipped with the same kinds of edges as downhill skis for turning and stopping ability. They are also wide, like back-country touring skis, and consequently weigh more than your typical touring ski. The more expensive they are, the stiffer the camber, for better control on downhill slopes. And they can be quite expensive, approaching the cost of downhill skis (I got mine on sale at the end of the season for less than I would have paid for a pair of light touring skis). Added to that cost is the investment in a heavy-duty binding and a sturdy boot, and you've got a $300 or $400 investment. But there's nothing quite like telemarking down a back-country bowl in perfect form, aided by the best equipment and, of course, many years' practice. Partial metal-edged skis are also available (the steel edges don't run the entire length of the ski), and are a good compromise between a lighter touring ski and a full metal-edge ski as they provide more control than the former but aren't as heavy as the latter. Don't choose the metal-edged skis until you've become a skier worthy of the technology. It's a waste of money otherwise.

Skins

For the experienced skier who prefers back-country skiing, skins are the way to go. Made of rubber or mohair, skins attach to the bottom of your skis to provide grip for climbing. Many skiers never wax their back-country skis but depend entirely on skins for the uphill terrain so that their skis are waxless—meaning faster—for the return run.

There are two different types of mohair skins—adhesive and nonadhesive. Adhesive skins come with a sticky surface that adheres to your ski. With normal use, you shouldn't have to reapply the glue more than once a year. Handling the skins is tricky, though, to keep the sticky surface clean and away from other items in your pack. The full length skins (they come in shorter lengths as well) retail at about eighty dollars.

The nonadhesive mohair skins are attached to your skis at the rear with a clip that must be pre-mounted on your ski, and manually clipped onto the tip. The mohair surface against the snow provides for both uphill grip and some glide for a steep downhill descent. The full length skins also retail for about eighty dollars.

Snakeskins, made of rubber, are the least costly, at about forty dollars retail. They attach to the ski with clips at the rear and tip, and can sometimes be difficult to stretch in cold weather They also provide no glide for downhill, but otherwise work well.

Poles

Most poles these days are made of fiberglass or metal for strength and durability. Bamboo poles (to match your wooden skis) are still available in some stores, but they break more easily than the fiberglass poles.

There are a few guidelines to follow in choosing a pole. The length of the pole is the distance from the floor to just under your armpit. The pole tip should be curved forward so that it pulls easi-

Example of child's touring skis with adjustable leather bindings

ly out of the snow. Synthetic pole baskets are replacing leather or bamboo ones. Choose a medium-size, flexible basket (as opposed to the larger bamboo ones and small, rigid ones) that is securely fastened to the pole. There's nothing more frustrating than skiing along in deep powder using your poles for balance when suddenly one of your poles sinks into the snow up to your armpit and over you go. I once spent an hour on the Winsor Trail digging through six feet of snow looking for a lost basket. Carry an extra pole basket in your pack and you won't have to do any digging.

Boots

Boot choice, like ski choice, is largely determined by the type of skiing you intend to pursue. Stiff, high-top boots that resemble downhill boots are for the back-country ski tourer or telemark skier who needs lots of foot and ankle support for distance and maneuverability. These boots usually have a groove in the heel for use with cable bindings, and can be equipped with a plastic notch for step-in bindings (discussed later). A heavy, high-quality boot is more important than a comparable metal-edged ski because without it you do not have the foot strength to control the heavy ski.

Most recreational skiers opt for a medium to light touring boot compatible with medium-weight touring skis. These come in a variety of styles and quality, but look for a fair amount of toe rigidity—how hard it is to hold the boot in your hand and twist the toe end back and forth—and good leather construction. Low-cut boots have been the most popular in recent years, allowing for freedom of movement, but the newer, higher-cut boots provide more ankle support and warmth. Racing boots are lightweight and low-cut, and in some cases, are simply a special track shoe for snow. Many racers are now using a racing shoe with an extended sole that fits into a special slot binding (discussed in the next section).

Bindings

Unlike downhill bindings, which lock you into a ski like a coyote caught in a trap, cross-country ski bindings are designed to facilitate freedom of movement, i.e., uphill climbs as well as downhill glides. Cross-country bindings are some form of toe binding, where the front part of your boot locks into position and your heel is free for walking and climbing. A cable binding, which loops around the back of the boot and secures your heel to the ski, is used primarily in back-country, downhill skiing where you want better lateral control of your skis for turns and stops.

Most toe bindings are of the pin binding variety (usually 75 millimeter). There are three metal pins or pegs on a metal plate that fit into three holes on the sole of the boot at the toe; a clamp locks the top of the sole at the toe onto these pegs. The kinds of clamps may vary, but the pin bindings all work basically the same way, and work well, providing good lateral control. They are also inter-changeable, which makes renting or borrowing skis possible.

Several other kinds of toe bindings are also available. Step-in bindings are closer to a downhill binding without the heel lock. The salomon binding, basically a racing binding, has become popular with ski tourers also. This binding requires a special boot with an extended sole at the toe, which slips into a slot on the binding. They are light and quick (a narrower binding, they produce less drag), but are, of course, not interchangeable with other toe binding models. Neither are they conducive to good turning technique as they provide less lateral control than the three-pin or step-in binding.

Cable bindings, which secure your heel, are usually accompanied by a release, like downhill bindings, to prevent injury. You can equip your boots with a V-notch that fits into a special metal plate on your ski when you need more control, or go to an even more sophisticated binding that secures your entire foot for downhill skiing in the back-country.

All skis should be equipped with a heel plate of some sort—

metal, plastic or rubber—which is attached to your ski right where your heel falls. This provides some friction between your heel and ski for better control and prevents snow buildup.

Care and Repair of Skis

PREPARATION

When it's that transitional time of year between the warm days of Indian summer and the steady winter snowstorms of January, get out your skis, start repairing any home-repairable gouges, and put on your base wax. That will make it seem like it's time to go skiing, at any rate. Fiberglass skis should be hot waxed—or base waxed—at the beginning of each snow season. You can do this with Alpine soft wax or glider wax (available at mountaineering stores) and an iron. Hold the wax against the iron, close to the ski; drip the wax along the two smooth sides of the ski next to the groove. Iron in the wax with a wool setting, smoothing it into the ski bottom as much as possible. After you've worked the wax in, let it cool and scrape off the excess wax, leaving a thin coat. Most ski stores will base coat your skis for you for a fee, but it's always a good idea to learn how to take care of your skis yourself.

Wood skis are prepared with some very sticky stuff called pine tar, which seals the bottoms and provides a good adherent for the different waxes you will apply over the season. Nowadays they sell spray-on pine tar, which makes the process incredibly easy, but does not last as long as the good old burn-it-in type.

If you want to mess with this base coating only once or twice a year, buy the liquid pine tar and a propane torch. Apply the tar with a small brush over the entire bottom surface of your ski. Then, with the torch, quickly run a flame over the ski (with the hot part of the flame at least six inches away from the wood) and you'll see the pine tar melt into the surface. When you've heated up the entire ski, rub off the excess pine tar with a rag. The surface should be just slightly sticky to the touch. If you're worried about burning your ski (and you should be) take your skis to the professionals for the first coating and watch how they do it.

You can also use the propane torch to remove gobs of wax left on your skis after a heavy day's waxing, on both wood and fiberglass skis. Again, use caution not to burn the surface.

If you have metal-edged skis you might want to take them into a ski shop at the beginning of the year to have the edges sharpened.

REPAIRS

Some repairs of both wood and fiberglass skis can be done at home. Gouges in fiberglass skis can be filled with a compound called Kofix candle, a soft plastic melted into the hole. Clean the hole first, melt the candle into the hole, then sand the surface smooth. Gouges in wood skis will usually disappear with a good scraping (I'm talking about a pile of wood shavings here). If after scraping some holes remain, fill them with plastic wood.

Delamination is when the layers of your ski start to separate. This is oftentimes caused by jamming your ski tails into snowbanks at lunchtime, so from now on lay them down or stand them up on top of the snow. To repair the ski, dry it thoroughly and gently spread open the delaminated area. Fill the spread with epoxy, as far up into the separation as possible, then squeeze the layers together, forcing out the excess epoxy. Wrap the area with waxed paper, use wooden splints on either side of the ski, and clamp. Be sure not to apply full pressure to the clamps until about an hour after you first put them on.

I was skiing with a class in the Peralta Canyon area when one of my group came zooming down off a connecting forest road straight into the crusty snowbank piled alongside the plowed road. Everyone knew by the noise of the resounding crack that she would be pulling her ski out tipless. Well, it wasn't exactly tipless—the tip was still there—but the cracks in her wooden ski rendered it useless. Rather than break off the tip at the crack and attach the fiberglass tip one of us carried in his pack, we decided to improvise and wrap the ski at the break so she could ski back to the car. We applied epoxy to the break, wrapped around the epoxy with plastic bags, and tied off the whole thing with the strings from someone's gaiters. She made it back to the car just fine, despite a few tears shed for her beautiful but broken wooden ski. I guess this serves as testimony to the advantages of the fiberglass ski, but she did go out and buy another pair of wooden skis.

If you do break your ski tip and this kind of repair isn't possible, you can secure a spare tip, equipped with edge grooves to slide over your broken ski, which will get you back to civilization. Spare tips are sold in most mountaineering and sporting goods stores.

STORAGE

After your last warm, slushy day of spring skiing, when you finally accept the fact that the season is over, leave a base coat of wax on your skis and find a nice, cool, dry wall to lean them up against (unblocked) to look at longingly until next year.

Waxing

If you have answered the profound question "to wax or not to wax?" in the negative you can skip this section, although I think it's a good idea for all cross-country skiers to have a working knowledge of waxing technique. You may find yourself on waxable skis someday, or in a group of skiers when your valuable knowledge saves the day for your friends on waxable skis.

I've already talked about base or glider waxing preparation for both fiberglass and wood skis. Now I'm going to talk about grip wax, or that seemingly endless supply of color-coded waxes applied over the base wax to accommodate various snow conditions. Perhaps the first thing you'd like to know is how a so-called "grip" wax works for skiing which includes both uphill and downhill terrain. The explanation goes something like this. Ski waxes allow microscopic irregularities in the snow to penetrate the waxed surface of the ski which maximizes friction for uphill climbs and minimizes friction for downhill glides. Understanding this basic principle, you must now figure out which kind of wax, from hard to soft, matches which snow condition, new or old, so that this principle remains operable.

As cross-country equipment becomes high-tech, so does the array of grip waxes available. Every snow condition has its matching wax, and as you become more experienced you'll be able to coordinate the two with greater facility. Fortunately, there is a standard color code that categorizes the waxes in a relatively understandable fashion: hard waxes for cold, new snow, are the cold colors white, green and blue; softer waxes for warmer, melted snow are the warmer colors purple, red, and yellow. There are also many "in-between" colors such as violet (between blue and purple), special green, harder blue, and softer blue. All these colors have air temperature ranges printed on the packages as a guideline, but experience is the best teacher for fine-line gradations.

APPLICATION

The hard waxes usually come in the form of small tins, and are rubbed, like a crayon, on the "kicker" zone of the ski. This kicker zone, where all grip waxes are applied, is the area of the ski directly beneath your foot, and an additional foot in length (approximately) in front and behind. This is the area that comes into the most contact with the snow. Skiers who want more purchase or grip can extend the kicker zone to include the whole ski. Racers sometimes shorten the zone to four or five inches.

Apply the wax to a clean, dry ski for best results. Cover the kicker zone with generous strokes of wax, then rub the wax out with a cork (sold with wax packages) to smooth out any gobs of wax. You can also use an iron or torch to heat the wax for application, but as you may be changing waxes throughout the day, miles from civilization, you'll obviously depend on this rub-and-cork method most often.

Klister wax, the consistency of toothpaste, is used for snow that has melted and refrozen. It comes in a color-coded tube and is very messy to work with. Warm up the tube to make it squeezable, and apply a thin line of this gooey stuff down each side of the groove along the kicker zone. Smooth the klister out with the plastic spatula that is usually sold with the tubes. You have more control over the spread of the klister with the heel of your hand, but if you're applying it out in the woods you're not going to want to ski around for the rest of the day with sticky hands. You can also apply the klister with a torch.

WAXING VARIABLES

To choose the day's wax, a hard wax or klister, assess the snow conditions, take the air temperature, and read the labels on the color-coded tins or tubes to find out which wax corresponds. If you are unsure which wax to choose—a blue or purple, for example—pick the harder, as it is much easier to apply a softer wax over a harder wax. If you do choose the purple, then the temperature drops and it starts to snow, necessitating a harder wax, scrape off the purple wax with a metal scraper and apply the blue wax. If you need to change klisters, you will probably have to scrape off the harder klister to apply a softer klister, due to the sticky nature of the stuff.

Beginners might want to forget the whole business and go for the two-wax system which is on the market. One wax (gold in the Swix system) is for cold days of dry, powdery snow; the other, silver, is for wet, packed snow above freezing temperatures. You can adjust to the subtle gradations between these two classifications by applying thin layers of wax to correspond to the cold, hard waxes, and a thick, rougher wax coat for the kind of slushy snow that calls for klisters. This two-wax system sometimes actually works better for that frustrating time when the snow condition changes right at the freezing point and a blue, purple, or violet wax won't keep your skis from icing up. One of the most frustrating experiences I ever had was skiing out of San Antonio Hot Spring in the Jemez Mountains. A class and I had had a lovely trip into the spring on beautiful new snow, and had enjoyed a hot bath just as it began to snow again. We looked forward to an easy trip out on more good snow, but almost immediately everyone started having trouble with icing and snow accumulation on our skis. Most of us stopped and rewaxed with violet or purple, guessing that the temperature must be near the troublesome 32° mark, despite the thickly falling snow. Things only got worse, though, as we came off the trail onto the forest road, and my skis started building up so much snow I felt like I was skiing on platform sandals. Finally, in desperation, someone suggested we try the gold from the two-wax system, and we managed to finish the last mile only stopping one more time to scrape off snow. The instructor was duly humbled.

As demonstrated by this San Antonio Hot Spring trip, snow conditions can always change in a matter of hours, and you'll have to change your waxes accordingly. Other variables that call for rewaxing are drastic terrain changes; for example, leaving open terrain where the sun is starting to melt the snow requiring a softer wax, and entering a shady trail where a harder wax is called for. You should initially wax for the prevailing condition, and either slip a little in the meadow or stick a little in the woods. You can anticipate both conditions by actually applying a hard wax lightly over a frozen klister (disregarding the rule of soft over hard).

Even if you find that one kind of wax is sufficient for a whole day's skiing, sometimes you must stop and rewax, especially in rough terrain. Icy, granular snow is the most abrasive, and calls for more frequent waxing. You can use a binder wax, a stickier version of klister, under hard waxes to help keep the wax on your skis.

GENERAL RULES OF THUMB

- If you continually slip on uphills your wax is too hard or you didn't put enough on. First wax a longer kicker area with the same wax, then change to the next softer wax.
- If you are not getting enough glide, you have either too soft a wax, or again, you didn't put on enough wax to start with. Scrape off the softer wax and go to the next harder one.
- Use klisters for snow that has melted and refrozen. Generally, red and yellow are soft klisters for really sloppy snow; blue and green klisters are for colder conditions; silver is in between.
- Beginning skiers can lengthen the kicker zone for more grip and less slippery skis.
- Those of you seeking the downhill thrill can shorten the kicker zone. For speed you can apply glider wax to the tip and tail of the ski.
- Wax for the prevailing condition of the day, using the predicted average temperature as a guide.
- Apply the wax to a warm, dry ski, then set the skis outside to cool before using.
- Experiment. Try breaking the old cardinal rule of only softer wax over hard wax, and try using klister/hard-wax combinations for unusual conditions. Then remember what you've used successfully for future reference.

Clothing

Just as equipment has become high-tech, leaving the natural materials behind for the synthetics, so has clothing. Polypropylene, a plastic, is the name of the game today. It may look and feel like cotton, but it is indeed a plastic. It was first employed in the manufacture of long underwear, an essential for cross-country skiing, and caught on fast because it is nonabsorbent and helps keep your skin dry of sweat (the moisture is pushed through to the next layer so the material next to your skin is always dry). Now it's used for everything else, too—socks, turtlenecks, pants, gloves, etc.—but that doesn't mean you have to array yourself from head to foot in plastic. There are some alternatives, from the inside out.

UNDERWEAR

Start with long underwear, tops and bottoms, polypropylene if you wish, or any other material that breathes. Duofold (a double layer of wool and cotton) underwear is good, and is actually made to look nice, too, if you strip down to your underwear (on top, that is) as the day warms up. Silk underwear has become popular, and feels especially nice next to your skin.

TOPS AND PANTS

The rule of thumb here is loose and comfortable. There's a lot of body movement in cross-country skiing—swinging arms and legs—and you need clothing that's not going to interfere. Knickers are the traditional cross-country favorite, and provide good leg freedom and style. Wool ones are best, as wool is also nonabsorbent, like polypropylene. These last few years you've probably seen more and more cross-country skiers outfitted like alpine skiers, in waterproof nylon ski outfits, or in the Spandex and Lycra of the racing world. I haven't crossed over that far yet (in fact, I hate the stuff), but waterproof pants definitely come in handy. A turtleneck of polypropylene or cotton goes over the long underwear on top. A roll-over collar provides good neck protection, and oftentimes this will be all you need for a comfortable day's skiing.

OUTER LAYERS

The rule of thumb on outer layers is not to overdress and sweat so much that when you stop to rest you immediately become cold from the sweat of too many clothes. If the day demands more than a pair of knickers and turtleneck, or nylon ski suit, bring along a lightweight windbreaker, ski vest, or wool sweater for added warmth. A down vest will provide sufficient warmth without inhibiting movement. It is not often that you will find you need a regular down parka. It's too bulky, and as you warm up with exertion you'll find you are too warm in the coat. I have a favorite rag wool sweater that fits loosely and comfortably, and is bright red so none of my students can miss me up ahead on the trail. Outfitters now sell lightweight fleece jackets that are almost as warm as wool and weigh less.

SOCKS

If you're wearing knickers you'll be wearing knee socks, too, of course. These come in the ubiquitous polypropylene, wool, or wool/ nylon combination, to shed water (most skiers wear gaiters as well, described below) If it's a cold day I wear a short pair of socks underneath my knicker socks, either polypropylene or silk. And if it's a miserable day, I've been known to sport a pair of rag-wool socks over my knicker socks.

For those of you who suffer from extremely cold-sensitive feet, sometimes diagnosed as "chillblains," you must take extra precautions to keep your feet warm while skiing. Usually the result of exposure to near frostbite conditions, chillblains are caused by damaged tissue that will never be healed. One of my friends who suffers from chillblains described her precautionary foot-dressing ritual to me. First, she rubs pure lanolin all over her feet, then puts on silk socks with cayenne pepper in the toes, and lastly wears at least two pairs of wool socks. She also warns cold sufferers to be sure that their ski boots are nice and roomy, as cramped toes are more susceptible to cold (and she recommends acupuncture treatments to help restore circulation). Chemically activated heat packs (for feet or hands) are sold in outdoor stores.

Several other ski accouterments help keep your feet warm, a most essential condition for good skiing:
• Gaiters fit over the top of your boot and extend up the leg in various lengths. Usually made of Gore-tex and nylon, they help keep the snow out of your boot and also protect your legs if you are skiing in deep snow or powder.

- Boot gloves are rubber boot coverings that slip over most toe-pin style boots.
- Sno-seal for your boots keeps them waterproof.

GLOVES OR MITTENS

Manufacturers now make glove linings of polypropylene that look like they were designed for Michael Jackson. These can be worn underneath nylon or Gore-tex mitten shells. Wool mittens can also be worn under nylon shells. Insulated gloves with thinsulate, polypropylene or foam are easier to keep track of. Down-lined mittens are often too bulky and warm, but I have skied on days when I was very glad I had them. Mittens of any kind generally work better than gloves, as finger contact is just like body contact, the warmest there is. If you are a beginner, and anticipate a lot of falling (as you should), be sure your gloves or mittens are waterproof and come down far enough over your wrists to prevent wet, cold, miserable hands.

HATS

If you don't know by now that you lose a significant amount of body heat through your head, remember the old adage, "When your feet are cold, put on a hat." There's always room in your day pack for a hat or two, so bring along a wool hat, your favorite cap, earband, or whatever.

Day Pack

This book is geared to the day ski tour versus the back-country, multi-day trek, so I will confine my pack essentials to what you will need for a single day's trip. I will mention some emergency equipment you might want to carry, as it is always best to be prepared for any contingency.

FOOD

Lunchtime can be the highlight of the day, especially if you've chosen an awe-inspiring spot and brought along delicious, mouth-watering food to replenish your energy stores. You work up a big appetite cross-country skiing, and you deserve the best. (Remember to plan your trip, if at all possible, so that most of the uphill climbs are accomplished before lunch, and the downhill glides afterward).

I bring along a good source of protein for the main course—cold chicken, salami and cheese, a hearty salad or peanut butter sandwich if you're a vegetarian—complemented by hard-boiled eggs, vegetable sticks, nuts, pickles, olives, bread, or pasta. Some folks bring a thermos of hot soup to add a touch of warmth, which is fine for day trips where bulky pack items are possible. Dessert usually means something very rich and sweet, which I normally don't eat, but skiing is a good rationale for indulgence. You don't have to overdose on sugar, however, and fresh or dried fruit may be a better choice to avoid over filling when there are miles yet to be skied. High-energy snacks should be included, too—fruit, sunflower seeds, sucking candy, nuts—to keep you going throughout the day. In class groups I like to celebrate a final outing by assigning each member a food item to share in a communal meal laid out on ponchos or space blankets. It heightens the camaraderie shared in cross- country skiing.

LIQUID

Bring along at least a quart of liquid in a plastic bottle for a day's excursion. Most people bring water, but I prefer something with some tang to it—juice, herbal tea, lemonade, gatorade, etc. You can pack a small thermos of soup, tea. or coffee if you don't mind the extra weight. It's definitely not a good idea to fill your canteen with wine instead of water, but I see nothing wrong with adding a shot of rum to your coffee. You do lose body fluids as you work up a sweat skiing, so even if you don't feel particularly thirsty be sure to drink your allotted liquid to keep from getting

Lunchtime on the trail

dehydrated.

PROTECTION

This was discussed in the clothing section as either a windbreaker, vest, or sweater. It's nice if any extra clothing can fit into your day pack so you aren't encumbered with sweaters or jackets tied around your waist to catch on trees or get lost in a snowbank.

EXTRA GLOVES, SOCKS AND HAT

I always bring along extras of all these items in case the ones I have get lost or wet, or one of my friends or students forgets to bring his or hers.

SUNSCREEN

The sun's rays are powerful, especially reflected off snow, and you need to protect your exposed skin. Remember, too, that your skin can burn on a cloudy day, and apply sunscreen whenever you go on a tour.

SUNGLASSES OR GOGGLES

The reflection of the sun off snow can also be harmful to your eyes, and you need to protect them as well as your skin. If you wear sunglasses you might want to add a strap around the back of your head so you won't lose them in a fall. Goggles are sometimes necessary if you're skiing in a snowstorm, especially if you wear corrective glasses that you need to keep on.

WAXES

Bring along your entire arsenal of waxes; you never know what conditions you might encounter. Include a cork, scraper, spatula, and brush.

FIRST AID KIT

You can keep this relatively simple, including band-aids, moleskin for blisters, aspirin or ibuprofen, a rolled bandage and tape, scissors, first aid cream.

SPACE BLANKET

This lightweight, fireproof, insulating item can be carried along for bivouac emergencies, and can function as well as a nice waterproof pad to sit on at lunch.

REPAIR KIT

You never know when the unexpected might happen and you or a friend might break a ski or have a binding come loose. See that you carry these items among all of you: spare ski tip, spare pole basket, duct tape, pocketknife, mini-pliers and screwdriver, steel wool, epoxy, hose clamps (for a broken pole).

MATCHES

Be sure to keep these in a waterproof container, as wet matches don't do anyone any good.

COMPASS AND MAPS

Snow can often be disorienting, so it's a good idea to have a compass on hand (and know how to use it). You should always check a map before starting out in unfamiliar territory, to get a general feel of the area and to know the mileage entailed.

Section II. TECHNIQUE

Two big advantages of cross-country skiing over alpine skiing are not having to stand in lift lines and the ease of acquiring proficiency—and subsequently enjoyment. At the tender age of twelve I suffered the agonies of a week's alpine ski lessons, and then a four-year apprenticeship to become the hot-dogger I envisioned: schussing down the mogul-covered slopes under the chairlift, wowing the riders beyond belief. Now, in my mature years, I've given it all up for the peace and solitude of the back-country trek, and I've turned countless friends and students on to these same joys in a matter of hours. Not to say that challenges don't await the cross-country skier as he or she acquires more sophisticated skills, but cross-country skiing is essentially an approachable, "do-your-own-thing" sport where you can readily pick up the basic skills necessary to get you out into the woods and on your own.

I'm going to list some of those basic skills here and describe as best I can the techniques employed to achieve proficiency. First, here is a short list to help the beginner prepare both mentally and physically for the first day's outing:

• Go out with someone (preferably not a wife or husband) who knows what he or she is doing, and watch them to see what they do. Then let them watch you and tell you what to do.

• Make sure you are properly dressed, even if you plan on a lesson of short duration. You'll probably end up spending some time lying in the snow, so all those clothes I talked about before will come in handy.

• Pick your terrain carefully. If you're going to the Sandias, don't let someone convince you to start out on North Crest Trail because "it's really not that steep." Go to the Tram Service Road, perfect for beginners, and don't let anyone tempt you onto the Crest Trail until you feel fully prepared.

• When you become tired, stop, go back to the car, the restaurant, the campfire, or whatever, and take a breather or quit. You don't have to worry about impressing any chairlift riders out there.

Basic Cross-Country Stride

Go find a flat piece of land covered with snow. Get your friend or instructor to make a track in the snow, and turn yourself into a copycat, matching the instructor's stride.

What you will be doing is progressing from a walk to a jog in what is called the "diagonal stride," the cross-country skier's basic mode of movement. Start out by sliding your left leg forward while at the same time reaching forward with your right pole and planting it in the snow about the same distance forward as your

The basic cross-country stride

left foot. Use your right pole to push forward a little, while at the same time pushing off with your right leg. Then reach forward with your left arm, slide your right leg forward, and push off with your left leg. In other words, start walking, arms counterbalanced, only use your skis in a glide and your poles to help push. Relax, bend your knees a little, lean forward slightly over your skis, put some pressure on them, and go forward. You will soon catch the rhythm of it, the "step-glide," the swing of your body, the continuity of your forward motion. Watch the person up ahead, copy his or her stride, and then try speeding everything up a bit. Imagine that you're jogging across the snow, putting a lot of "kick" or pressure on the forward-moving ski. The rear ski will probably start lifting higher off the snow, like you've seen a racer's ski do, but don't concentrate on this too much, or try for their longer stride. Stick to a smooth, relatively short-stepped jog through the snow, and the embellishments will come later.

POLING

A little explanation of poling technique is in order next. Poles are not merely training wheels for balance, but an intricate part of your diagonal stride. Stick your pole into the snow in front of you, slanted forward at a slight angle, and just to the outside of where your opposite boot will be coming forward on your ski. This allows you to push on your pole, propelling your body forward, until the pole is then behind your hip, and the opposite pole swings forward to plant in the snow. Instructors often take away beginners' poles until they become proficient at the leg movements of the diagonal stride, as poles can sometimes confuse the issue—especially when beginners try to use them to stop.

I happen to use my poles quite a bit, and oftentimes have sore shoulders rather than sore legs after a long day's trip. This is perfectly all right, as long as you use your poles in conjunction with your stride. North Americans seem to rely more on their arms, as opposed to Europeans, whose soccer background emphasizes leg skills. As you become more comfortable in your diagonal stride, your arms will fall into rhythm too, swinging like pendulums, utilizing your shoulder and back muscles to propel you along.

DOUBLE-POLING

This technique can be used on flat or gentle downhill terrain-rain to give your legs a rest. Practice this in your first lesson along with the diagonal stride.

Try it first on level ground to see what kind of shape your shoulder muscles are in. Simply plant both poles in the snow alongside your parallel skis and push yourself forward. Continue to plant your poles and pull-push yourself across the snow with no leg movement. After you get used to keeping your balance on parallel skis (keep your skis about six inches to a foot apart, each ski directly under each hip), you can try this technique on a gentle hill and you'll have an idea what downhill skiing is all about.

Put your whole upper body into the double-poling technique and you will move right along across the meadow or down the hill.

FALLING

It is now time to talk about falling, which you will have already experienced practicing your diagonal stride (or trying to put your skis on, for that matter). Remember, there is nothing unusual about losing your balance when you suddenly find yourself trying to negotiate the simplest maneuvers on size 50 shoes. Also remember that snow conditions are rarely pristine, and your skis may slip out from under you without a moment's notice. Don't be afraid to fall—your pride will suffer more than your body.

As a beginner, traveling at slow speeds, you will usually fall backwards or sideways onto your rear or thighs. These areas of the body are usually well padded, and the snow provides a soft landing anyway. If you are a more experienced skier, traveling at greater speed, try to avoid falling forward, as that position is more apt to cause injury.

The correct way to fall—backwards

To get back up after you've fallen, first arrange your skis in a parallel position. If they are both stuck in the snow, sticking straight up in the air, this means rolling onto your back and lifting them over your head until they come together. Make sure they point across the fall line of the hill—fall line meaning the path of least resistance, or straight down the hill. Make sure your skis are on the downhill side of your body. There's nothing harder than trying to get up when your skis are pointed down the hill ready to carry you away. Next, get onto your knees, then stand up, pushing yourself with your hands. Some people use their ski poles planted in the snow to help push themselves up, but if you're a beginner, forget this maneuver for the time being. Hands and knees are steadier.

Uphill Skiing

This is what distinguishes the cross-country skier from the alpine skier, the notion that one can actually ski uphill and enjoy it. Instead of buying a $30 lift ticket for the privilege of riding uphill, you get to burn calories, expand lung capacity, and enjoy the satisfaction of achievement by skiing uphill. And remember, there's almost always a downhill on the flip side to compensate you for all your hard work.

Most of your uphill travel will be achieved with the diagonal stride, simply adjusting your speed to the incline of the slope, much like hiking. When the terrain becomes steep enough to require additional skills to prevent slipping, however, you must resort to various cross-country uphill techniques that allow you to master the hill.

JOGGING, OR ATTACKING THE HILL

The simplest way to get up a not-too-steep-but-steep-enough-to-cause-problems hill is to maintain your diagonal stride and just speed it up to a jog. Your momentum moves you up the hill. If you find that you are slipping, adjust to the diagonal-stride technique I call "attacking the hill." Shorten your stride and "stomp" your skis into the hill with real gusto. Keep your poles on a diagonal for best pushing power, and keep your body weight forward. You obviously can't keep up this kind of attack forever, so use this technique on short hills.

HERRINGBONE

When the slope of the hill becomes too steep to use the modified diagonal stride, you must resort to the herringbone. This is a rather slow and tedious method, but it actually looks more awkward than it is. Spread your skis into a V, the front tips wide open, the backs close together (a reverse snowplow, a technique I'll describe later). Use the inside edges of your skis for traction on the snow and waddle up the hill, alternating your arm and leg movements, as in the diagonal stride. Try not to make the V so wide that you have no grip or control, one of the first things beginners tend to do when faced with a hill they can't conceive of conquering. You can adjust the size of the V to anticipate narrow places on the trail or particularly steep sections where you need a wider stance.

SIDESTEPPING

This is the method of last resort, other than taking off your skis and walking. Stand with your skis across the fall line of the slope, turn your skis into the hill so your uphill edges grip the snow, and start sidestepping, the uphill ski first, followed by the other, up the hill. It helps your progress to point the tips of your skis slightly uphill so your ankles don't turn in too far and you lose your grip.

TRAVERSING—KICK-TURNING

Traversing is the easiest way of moving uphill in a wide, open area as opposed to a narrow trail. The layout of a traverse resembles that of a switchbacking highway, or a zig-zag across the slope

Herringbone

of a hill.

Stand with your skis across the fall line of the hill, and begin a diagonal ski line across and up the hill by moving your uphill ski forward and slightly uphill at the same time. Then slide the other ski alongside and ahead, and you will progress in an uphill and forward motion. When you get to the end of your switchback, and it's time to turn around to traverse the other direction, you can sometimes use a herringbone turn to get yourself pointed in the opposite direction (if there is room and the slope is not too steep). You may have to use a kick-turn to get the 180° change of direction you need, however. Don't be afraid of this seemingly complicated and precarious maneuver It's just a matter of balance and confidence, which you'll rapidly acquire after a few ungainly spills in the snow, with your skis crossed in the air or caught underneath each other in a foot of powder.

Try the kick-turn on the flats first. Decide which leg you want to lead the turn, then plant the corresponding pole forward and out of the way of the ski (left arm with left leg, right with right). Lift the tip of your ski straight up (not out to the side) until the whole ski is off the ground. Swivel the tip around to the outside in an arc until the ski is pointed in the opposite direction. You are now in the most uncomfortable ballet position invented, so quickly shift your weight onto the turned ski and bring the other ski around and over the turned ski so they both face in the same direction. Lift your planted pole as you bring the ski around or you'll impede the last procedure Now try it on a hill. Most people prefer starting the exercise with the uphill ski so you turn toward the hill, minimizing the danger of the out-of-control-one-legged-ski-down-the-hill trick. This is hard, though, if the slope is quite steep and you can't get your ski across the hill easily. Then you may have to turn facing downhill. If you're on that kind of hill in the first place, you're probably an expert skier anyway, so don't worry.

Sidestepping up a steep trail

Downhill Skiing

Now comes the real fun, learning the skills that enable you to experience an exhilarating run down a back-country trail or out ski an alpine skier on a downhill slope. By learning all these skills you'll be able to negotiate a wide range of terrain and pick your favorite style of skiing with the confidence you need for real cross-country fun. For many years I balked at the very idea of telemarking down the Sandia Peak Ski Basin, at odds with the philosophy of back woods cross-country skiing. But I finally succumbed and tried it out one day, picked up the telemark turn in a long practice session down the mountain (more or less—at least without falling) and immediately bought a one-way ticket back up the chairlift to do it all over again. So when I'm in a gregarious mood I play around at the ski area, and also hone my skills for back-country bowls where the telemark turn is an invaluable tool to cross-country touring. I'll begin this section with the cross-country techniques geared mainly to trail skiing, and work up to the telemark turn for more alpine-like skiing.

STRAIGHTAWAY

Pointing your skis straight down the hill and going for it is obviously the quickest way to get from point A to point B, but this also obviously has its drawbacks, especially when the trail descends at a 45° angle and there's a tree sitting at the bottom of it. If the slope is moderate, however, skiing straight down the trail is a good way for the beginner to learn body position and balance, and have some fun at the same time. Keep your skis hip-width apart, bend your knees slightly to lower your body weight, and let gravity do its job pulling you down the trail. Your poles should be slightly behind you, just off the snow, and close to your body to avoid snagging trees and rocks. In good snow conditions, and on a hill with enough slope to carry you without occasional strides to keep up speed, you can glide down the hill and get a feel for the essence of skiing, the speed, the balance, the ride with the wind.

Of course, you can start gaining too much speed and proceed to scare yourself out of your wits, so now it's time to learn the techniques to control this speed, as well as negotiate bumpy terrain, turns in the trail, and various obstacles (especially trees and other skiers).

STEP-TURN

The easiest way to follow the turn in the trail and avoid the big spruce tree ahead is to simply pick up the inside ski, point in the direction you want to turn, then lift the other ski over next to the first ski. This has to be accomplished fairly quickly, but as you practice you'll get the feel of it, and also modify the step-turn with a skate. This is accomplished by using the inside edge of the outside ski (the ski farthest away from the direction of your turn) to secure your position for the turn. Shift your weight to the inside ski as you point it in the direction of the turn, and push out in a skating motion with the outside ski to bring yourself around into the turn. This looks just like the skating you see on the ice and on alpine skis with metal edges. Both step-turns and skate-turns come in handy on trails with deep ruts and grooves carved by previous skiers. You can step into grooves for a straight run down the slope, or step out of ruts that are too deep and crusty.

SNOWPLOW STOPS AND TURNS

When the trail gets so steep that you want to slow down before you attempt a step-turn (or you just want to slow down, period), the snowplow does the trick.

From a straightaway position, push the rear of your skis out with your heels until you are in a wedge, tips facing toward each other about six inches apart. Sink your weight onto your thighs, drop your rear, and roll your ankles inward until the inside edges of your skis create enough friction to start slowing you down. In an effective snowplow you'll feel the drag on your knees and thighs as these muscles work to maintain a wedge and edge your skis.

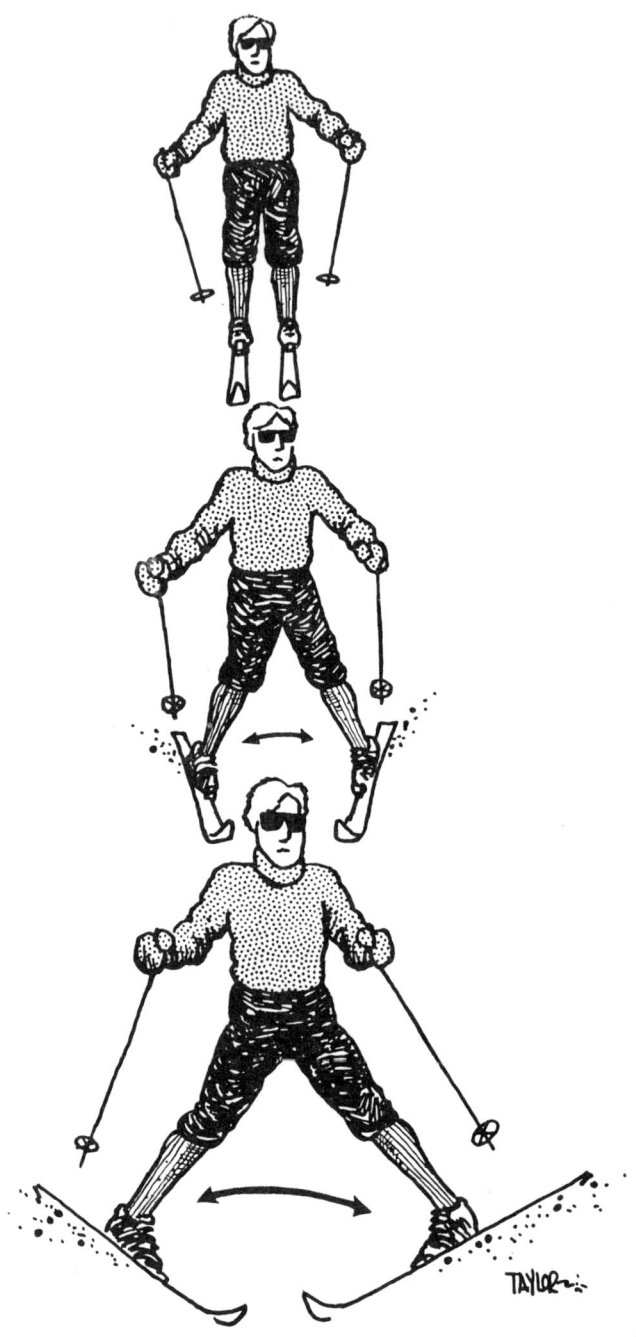

Snowplow

Snowplow turn

The wider the wedge, the more friction you create to slow down. If the slope is not too steep, you can wedge and edge until you come to a complete stop. Or you can use the snowplow, along with the snowplow turn, to negotiate the twists and turns of the trail.

To turn in either direction, shift your weight to the outside ski (remember, the ski farthest away from the direction you wish to turn) by bending your knee, push out with your heel, and turn your upper body the direction of the turn. This is not as impossible as it sounds. If you want to turn right, shift your weight onto the left ski, push out with your left heel into a wedge, point your knee and upper body to the right, and—voila—you will turn right. If you want to turn left, reverse the procedure. A good way to practice is to find an easy, open slope (the beginner slope at a downhill area) and start traversing the slope in a snowplow, turning at each side to practice both right and left turns.

STEM CHRISTIE

You may be saying, hey, wait a minute, stem christie is downhill terminology. But cross-country skiers can quite easily master a stem christie, which is simply a cross between a snowplow turn and the more difficult parallel turn, also of alpine vintage. You may want to practice this on an open slope before you tackle a twisting trail.

Traverse the slope with your skis together. Push or step into the wedge of the snowplow and begin your snowplow turn. Let's say you're turning to the left. Shift your weight to the right, and begin to come around to the left. When you are three-quarters of the way through the turn, simply lift your left ski (your weight is still on the right ski) and slide it over next to the right ski so you are in a parallel position again, ready to traverse back the other way across the slope. When you are out on the trail, you can correlate your speed, turn, and narrowness of the trail by utilizing a stem christie. It lets you head into the turn in a snowplow but quickly skid around into a parallel position before the turn is completed, ready to enjoy some more straightaway action.

OPEN SLOPE

All the turns and techniques previously discussed can be employed on the open slope that is too steep or full of moguls (little bumps and hills) to point your skis downhill and go for it. By

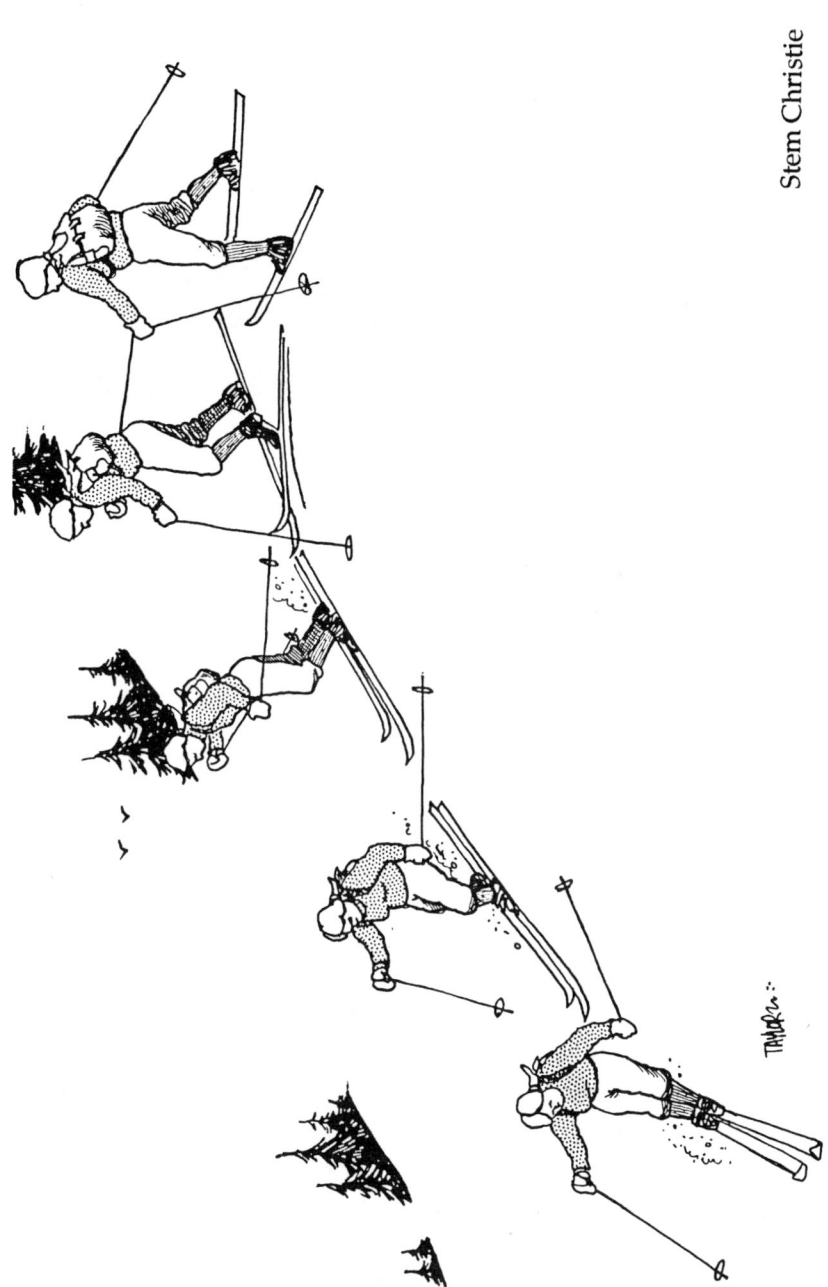

Stem Christie

combining all your skills you become a better, safer skier: ski down the smooth, gentle part of the slope; step-turn away from crusty, overused areas; snowplow to slow down as the slope increases; snowplow turn into a traverse across the fall line; stem christie turn in and out of your traverses, all the way down the mountain. Enjoy your control and the variation of your skills; this

A snowplow on the open slope

is your reward for all the uphill effort you just expended to reach this downhill thrill.

TELEMARK TURN

This is the graceful turn that is used by cross-country skiers on the alpine slopes. At any given downhill area you'll see telemarkers zooming down the most difficult slopes, impressing everyone with their speed and skill. Actually, telemark skiing was invented a long time ago as the best method for cross-country skiers in Telemark, Norway, to negotiate deep powder slopes. With the advent of the lock-in heel binding, the telemark turn, dependent upon the heel-lift movement of cross-country bindings, was replaced by the

Telemark turn

parallel stem turn. Now, the telemark turn is returning with a vengeance, as cross-country and mountaineering skiers recognize its usefulness and enjoy its grace. It is easier to execute now, too, with the advent of metal-edged, specially cambered skis. The telemark turn essentially works by creating one long ski as you extend one leg in front of the other in a diagonal stride. Body weight is distributed evenly, half on the front ski, half on the rear ski. Your body weight is low, with both knees bent into a half-crouch, the rear knee almost touching the snow. The rear weight rests on your toe, heel raised. This is not the *en garde* position where you lunge forward to stab your opponent. It's a 50-50 proposition, front and rear ski.

After you've got the balance of one ski extended and your weight properly distributed, the turn is accomplished by edging the front ski and pointing the knee in the direction of the turn (just like in a snowplow turn). If you are turning left, extend the right ski forward, edge to the inside, sink down on both skis, and follow your right knee around to the left. Your poles should be counterbalanced, the left pole forward to compensate for the left ski to the rear.

More than likely, you've just completed your first telemark fall. This turn does not feel natural right away, but as you learn the essential ingredients, and progress to linked telemark turns down the hill, the feeling is akin to graceful flying. Start out on a relatively, moderate slope and practice half-telemark turns into the hill. When you get used to the weight distribution, and the fact that this position will actually cause you to turn, you can progress to slightly steeper traverses where you can complete 180° turns. To link turns you will have to ski straighter down the hill to acquire the speed necessary for the more parallel telemark. Your body rises up and out of each turn, quickly sinks down into position as you shift your skis and weight, and your skis steer you through a rhythmic arc down the mountain.

Skating

This technique, described in the section on step-turns, is becoming more and more prevalent, especially with racers who have discovered that it is faster than the diagonal stride on certain terrain (especially the Tram Service Road in the Sandias, which skaters have just about taken over). As stated before, skating is essentially that—using your skis as skates to glide from side to side as you push off, left then right, along wide, fairly level terrain (you can also skate downhill to increase your speed). Most skaters use their poles on only one side, to push from behind, although you can use your poles to push from behind, right pole with left ski, left pole with right ski, as in a diagonal stride. You'll soon find a rhythm that enables you to enjoy the speed of skating.

Section III. SAFETY

HYPOTHERMIA

Hypothermia is the lowering of the inner-core body temperature due to exposure to cold, windy, or wet conditions. Symptoms include shivering, fatigue, disorientation, numbness, slow pulse, blue lips, slurred speech, etc. If not treated immediately, the body temperature can descend irreversibly. Treatment includes taking the victim to shelter, removing wet clothing, and warming with a fire, sleeping bag, body heat, or hot bath.

Pay attention to the prevention of hypothermia and you won't have to worry about the treatment. Know your skiing skills and your limitations. Don't take off on a ski trip with more experienced skiers who want to ski more miles than you think you are capable of skiing. Don't adopt the attitude that reaching your goal or destination is worth all cost. I once went out to the Jemez Mountains to explore a trail to take my classes on. It had snowed the night before, but the first half of the trail had already been skied, and I followed an easy track to the descent into the canyon. Here the broken trail stopped, however, and I was skiing on pristine, unbroken snow. My dog was with me and I had to stomp the snow with each step so he wouldn't sink up to his belly. I was determined to find the shortcut back to the road rather than backtrack the way I'd come, but I finally decided that, if I was already at the point where the route back was as much as I could handle, I'd better indeed turn back in case I never found the shortcut. I would have been stuck out in the snow for the night with no sleeping bag or shelter. I wisely chose retreat.

Also, if you are an inexperienced skier, don't ski by yourself unless it's outside your door through familiar terrain. If you are an experienced skier and enjoy skiing alone, always let someone know your route of travel and when you expect to return.

AVALANCHES

Most day-tour skiers need not worry about avalanche danger, although in heavy snowfall years avalanches have occurred in unusual places. On slopes of 35°-45,° avalanches sometimes happen when the snowfall is too great for the terrain holding it in place. They usually occur on open slopes, but sparse timber is sometimes not sufficient to hold the snow. Check with the Forest Service to find out about potential avalanche areas. Warnings will usually be posted at the specific site. During the last few years avalanche warnings have appeared on trails in the Wheeler Peak area near Taos. If you plan on skiing back-country terrain where avalanches have occurred, the best preparation is to take an avalanche course to learn the types of snow that most often precipitate avalanches, and the proper equipment to take with you.

BIVOUAC

Although with careful planning you'll probably never have to contend with an unexpected overnight stay (bivouac) on the trail, here is some helpful information, just in case. If it becomes obvious that you are not going to reach your car or planned shelter because of exhaustion, injury, or losing your way, stop before it gets dark to make camp. This may be a hard decision at best, to realize you must stop, but you cannot risk suffering hypothermia wandering around in the dark. The best protection for the night is a snow cave—a hollowed area in the snow that provides insulation and protection from the wind. If that's not possible, it's best to stay in the trees and assemble some sort of lean-to shelter with your skis and tree boughs.

Build a fire that can be kept going all night. Take turns tending the fire throughout the night, watching that the others resting don't get too chilled or accidentally burned. Be sure to drink plenty of water to avoid dehydration, and eat your food throughout the night for extra calories. If you've brought your space blanket along, you'll have a ready-made bed for the snow. And if you've told someone where you were going, chances are they'll be out looking for you. Don't panic. Many cross-country skiers have survived many nights in completely adverse conditions.

FROSTBITE

Frostbite is not as potentially dangerous as hypothermia, as it affects the extremities rather than the inner body core, but it can result in amputation. Symptoms are first a prickly feeling in your fingers or toes, then pain, then numbness. The skin will turn pale, and in the worst cases, white. If the initial symptoms are recognized before frostbite sets in, you can warm the extremities by putting them under armpits or against the bare skin of skiing partners. Do not rub the affected area, submerge in hot water, or put close to a fire. If the frostbite is severe, only trained medical personnel should treat it.

GETTING LOST

If you have planned your ski trip well and carry maps and compass with you, it's unlikely you will get lost. Sometimes, however, due to bad weather—white-outs, blizzards—or inattention, you will find yourself off the trail and unsure which way to go. If you do become lost and are without a compass, follow these general rules:
1. Stop and regroup. When you first suspect you are lost, don't push on undaunted, but stop, talk things over, and plan a course of action.
2. Backtrack. Follow your ski tracks back from where you came and you'll probably find where you lost the trail.
3. If you are hopelessly off the trail, follow the natural features of the land: streams and canyons will almost invariably lead you back to highways and civilization.
4. Don't search until you are exhausted. Stop, bivouac, and wait for the search party to find you.

ALTITUDE SICKNESS

This usually occurs above 7,000 feet and is characterized by dizziness, headache, shortness of breath, lack of energy, and nausea. If you begin to feel sick, stop, rest, drink fluids, eat some high-energy food, and return to lower elevations. The best prevention is to be sure you're in good physical condition and accustomed to a climate and altitude before you set off on a strenuous ski tour.

PHYSICAL CONDITIONING

This is one of the most important factors contributing to an enjoyable, safe ski tour. If you're not in reasonably good physical condition, a six- to ten-mile tour will become an ordeal rather than the treat it should be. If you are an active, physically fit person all year round, cross-country skiing is a rewarding winter sport that helps keep you in good shape. If winter is approaching and you've been sitting around all fall waiting for it, I recommend you get in shape before you hit the slopes and trails. At least twenty to thirty minutes of exercise three to five times a week—walking, jogging, swimming, bicycling, racquetball, basketball, anything to get your cardiovascular system going—at least a few months before it snows is necessary to avoid injury and fatigue on ski tours. Exercise for the sake of exercise is anathema to many people (and really not the point), so stay in shape all year round with appropriate sports for each season, preferably those that get you outside and don't cost too much money. You can always hike in the mountains until it's time to put your skis on and ski in the mountains.

It's also important to limber up before each day's ski tour even if you are already in good shape. Do some stretching exercises in the morning before you leave the house, or as you leave the car at your ski site, to warm up those stiff muscles. Limber muscles are less likely to be injured in falls and twists.

Section IV. SKIING WITH CHILDREN

We started both our kids on skis when they were four years old, so I can say from experience that this is one instance where it's OK to let a four-year old dictate the terms. Let them decide where they want to go, how far they want to go, and with whom they want to go. And when they're ready to stop, by all means let

Nancy with baby Marie in a front pack

them take off their skis and play in the snow—maybe you can even get in a little skiing while they're flopping in the snow making angels.

EQUIPMENT

For very young children, under age five or six, you can purchase ski sets that have adjustable bindings for regular snow boots. These bindings come attached to the skis and are usually constructed of plastic or leather straps with buckles so that your child can wear his or her regular snow boot. It will be bad enough in years to come trying to keep up with changing three-pin boot sizes every other year. The skis are quite short for easier maneuvering, with patterned bottoms, and the sets usually come with poles as well.

As your child grows out of these first ski sets, I recommend going to a regular child's ski with pattered bottom and three-bin binding. Corresponding three-bin boots in assorted sizes are usually easy to come by, either new in the outdoor stores, or used at ski swaps or any of the second-hand sporting good shops. Many of these shops will take trade-ins as you move up to a new size, but if you have multiple children you may want to hang on to all your out-grown boots for the next kid in line. Poles are measured the same way you would for an adult and should come up to the child's armpit.

CLOTHING

It's imperative that a child stay warm while skiing, for safety's sake and for fun's sake. Dress your child in layers, just as you would yourself. Long underwear for children may be hard to find, but you can always use sweatpants and a turtleneck in its stead. A wool sweater goes next, if it's cold, and then the all-important snowsuit, which usually consists of bib overalls and a matching jacket of waterproof material. If the day warms up as you ski, you can always take the child's coat off and the bib will still keep him or her dry during many falls in the snow.

The child should wear a liner sock and wool sock in the snow boot, even if the boot is insulated or padded. Children always manage to get snow inside their boots, or even lose them altogether. Waterproof, insulated (down or thinsulate) mittens that fit correctly are often hard to find for young children, but kids can always put their entire hand into too-large mittens rather than struggle with the thumb hole. Always take along several pairs, or a wool pair and insulated pair to exchange during changing weather conditions. Attach them to the sleeves of the coat to prevent the missing mitten routine.

A wool hat, or face mask, rounds out the picture of the bundled child who can barely move but is ready to embark upon his or her first skiing adventure.

PLANNING

If you're lucky enough to live in northern New Mexico like we do, then you can take a fool-proof ski trip out your front door with your kids. Otherwise, plan on a trip that takes you not far from home, or someplace where the kids can find warmth and shelter once they begin to tire. You'll see many kids skiing the Tram Service Road in the Sandia Mountains, as it's only $1^{1}/_{2}$ miles to the restaurant, where everyone can take a break before the return trip to the car. We took our son Jakob up to the D.H. Lawrence Ranch, near San Cristobal, on one of his first ski trips, where we could ski out our cabin door.

Choose level terrain for the first outing. The first several ski lessons will consist of getting your kids used to walking around with these huge things on their feet, and the last thing they need to worry about is sliding down a hill. Try to make sure your first outing is after a good snow, so the kids aren't slipping on ice and crusty snow.

It's also a good idea to take along your child's friend, if possible. This serves two purposes: children almost always have more fun in any activity with someone their own age; and the kids always seem to lend each other moral support (or perhaps it's just

Max, four-years old, skiing out the door of the house

the competitive edge) when they're trying something new together. If you can manage to take along another set of parents as well, all the better.

Finally, let the kids determine how long you stay out. There will inevitably be a certain amount of whining and complaining from the outset, but once it becomes serious whining and complaining, it's futile to try to continue skiing. You want the first ski trips to be fun, not or ordeal—for the parents or the kids.

LESSONS

For the most part, skiing with young children is getting them used to the skis and the snow and trying to have some fun. But there are a few things to keep in mind to help them learn basic cross-country technique—unless you just turn them over to the professionals and be done with it.

Start them out on level terrain so they can simply walk with the skis on. Downhill ski instructors always start kids out with no poles, but I've found that on cross-country skis most kids instinctively know how to use their poles for balance as they're getting used to being on skis. Later, when you're trying to teach them some downhill skills, you can take their poles away so they don't rely on them for stopping.

Once the kids feel comfortable on the skis, you can try showing them the herringbone technique for walking uphill. This will take some time, of course, as they cross their skis, fall down, and get frustrated, but once they actually start "walking like a duck" and manage to make it up the hill they'll be quite proud of themselves.

Next, find a slightly inclined hill, make a track, and have them try skiing your track. Remind them to bend their knees and lean slightly forward—kids always tend to lean backwards on their skis when going downhill, losing their balance. After trying this a few times, you can find a slightly steeper hill, put your child between your legs (without poles), hold her under the shoulders, and take her down the hill with you for a little downhill thrill. We actually did this with Max, our youngest, on a downhill run his first time out, and while my legs and back were killing me by the time we got down, he had a great time.

Once they get a feel for moving downhill on the skis you can teach them the snowplow. Again, this will take some time to accomplish, so be patient and don't be disappointed if it takes two or three outings before they achieve their first effective wedge. Remind them to stay down low, bend their legs, and push out with their skis. Sometimes older kids actually get the feel of the snowplow more quickly than adults, as they're already closer to the ground and have better balance.

Section V. SKI TRAILS

The following cross-country ski trails include some of my favorite northern New Mexico tours, described in detail, and a listing of additional trails in the same areas as the described tours. The trails are categorized by national forest and mountain range, and include both beginning excursions of two to three hours' duration and more advanced tours that may take all day.

At the beginning of each trail description I have listed the average elevation of the tour, mileage of the round trip, and the degree of difficulty. **Class I** trails are those with little elevation gain, appropriate for novice and beginner skiers. **Class II** trails contain more difficult terrain, including ascents and descents, and require the ability to negotiate stops and turns. **Class III** trails are for the more experienced skier whose technique and good physical condition enable him or her to handle the steeper, winding, narrow trail conditions, as well as an eight- to twelve-mile distance. The distance of the described tours varies from two to twelve miles, the latter distance being about as far as a day-tour skier wants to venture. While the scope of this book is not meant to cover all the necessary information for overnight ski excursions, any of the tours can be turned into overnight adventures (with the proper planning and equipment, of course).

I have tried to include enough detail in my ski tours to ensure that the skier feels comfortable enough, and knowledgeable enough, to travel in unfamiliar terrain without fear of getting lost. When I was learning new routes I used a less detailed guidebook, and often found myself completely confused and resorting to educated guesses—or just plain winging it. Some of us always feel that primitive desire to explore new, virgin territory as our predecessors did years ago in the wild mountains of New Mexico, but as this is the 1990s and these mountains are traveled and documented at every turn, our adventures must revolve around the fact that the trail is new to us, and just as beautiful and inspiring as it was to the first humans who ever climbed Truchas Peak or Mount Taylor. And if you are going to be out there in unpredictable elements, you might as well be sure of where you're going.

In choosing your day tour from the following list of trails, be sure to consider these factors:

1. How experienced are the skiers in your group? If everyone is at the most advanced level of expertise, then you can choose one of the more difficult routes and assume that everyone is going to be able to easily ski it and have a good time. If one or two of the people in the group are not as experienced, or not in the same shape, you should choose your tour with these people in mind. An over-taxing tour will be no fun for them, and your fun will be diminished by guilt at not being a responsible leader. Many times in my classes I have to cope with a diversity of skills within the range of both beginner and intermediate groups, and while I've never had to leave anyone on the trail, I've felt badly if someone in the class obviously had a miserable time trying to keep up with the rest of us. More importantly, it's dangerous to push someone beyond his or her limit, as that's what causes accidents or life-threatening situations.

2. What kind of terrain is included on the tour, and how many miles can you safely ski in a comfortable day? If everyone in the group is in fairly good shape, you can usually ski at least two miles an hour on variable terrain, for five or six hours. Remember, however, that an unbroken trail takes more time to ski. Take turns breaking trail so no one person in the group is stuck with all the work. Many years ago I skied with a friend down the North Crest Trail in the Sandias, from the Tramway to Placitas. Once we skied past the Cañon del Agua Overlook the trail was unbroken, with new snow falling all the time. I was in the lead, and as I looked back at my friend I began to wonder why I was step-gliding in the diagonal stride while she was double-poling in a fairly effortless glide down

the mountain. We both had the same wax on our skis, even the same type of skis, so I was mystified. Finally, about midway through the switchbacks on the east side of the mountains we stopped to rest, and then she took the lead. Voila—there I was gliding down the hill, free and easy, while she plodded along up ahead. An obvious observation—unbroken snow is harder to ski on than broken snow. Unfortunately, we soon traded positions again, as we realized I was the stronger skier and was going to have to break trail if we expected to reach Placitas intact, and before dark. I was sore for two days.
3. Take into account the weather. If it's the middle of the winter, overcast, and likely to storm (or is storming), you're probably not going to want to drive fifty miles on snow-packed roads to a ten-mile tour. Fresh snow can be the cross-country skier's ultimate dream, but driving time and trail-breaking time need to be considered. Also, you're going to have to expend a lot of energy just staying warm, and may subsequently deplete the energy needed to ski the ten or twelve miles. If it's a nice, warm, spring day, remember the nature of the terrain—exposure, slope, etc.—and choose a tour where the trail will still provide adequate conditions for good skiing.

Abbreviations

CG:	campground
ft:	feet
FR:	national forest road
FT:	national forest trail
Mt.:	mountain
N:	north
NM:	New Mexico highway
Spr.:	spring
US:	U.S. highway

Forest Service Offices

CIBOLA NATIONAL FOREST
Supervisor's Office
2113 Osuna Road NE
Albuquerque, NM
(505) 761-4650

Sandia Ranger District
11716 Highway 337
Tijeras, NM 87059
(505) 281-3304

Mountainair Ranger District
P.O. Box E
Mountainair, NM 87036
(505) 847-2990

Mount Taylor Ranger District
1800 Lobo Canyon Rd.
Grants, NM 87020
(505) 287-8833

SANTA FE NATIONAL FOREST
Supervisor's Office
1220 St. Francis Drive
Santa Fe, NM 87504
(505) 988-6940

Jemez Ranger District
P.O. Box 98
Jemez Springs, NM 87025
(505) 829-3535

Cuba Ranger District
Cuba, NM 87013
(505) 289-3265

Pecos Ranger District
P.O. Box 429
Pecos, NM 87552
(505) 757-6121

Las Vegas Ranger District
1926 N. 7th Street
Las Vegas, NM 87701
(505) 425-3534

CARSON NATIONAL FOREST
Supervisor's Office
208 Cruz Alta Road
Taos, NM 87571
(505) 758-6292

Camino Real Ranger District
P.O. Box 348
Peñasco, NM 87553
(505) 587-2255

Taos Ranger District
P.O. Box 558
Taos, NM 87571
(505) 758-2911

Questa Ranger District
P.O. Box 110
Questa, NM 87556
(505) 586-0520

Tres Piedras Ranger District
P.O. Box 728
Tres Piedras, NM 87577
(505) 758-8678

Map Legend

Trail	▬ ▬ ▬ ▬
Intermittent Stream	▬ · ▬ · ▬
Dirt road	═══════
Paved road	▬▬▬▬▬▬
Picnic ground or campground	⌂
Peak	▲
Spring	⸮

Unless otherwise indicated, maps are oriented north at the top of the page.

CIBOLA NATIONAL FOREST

Sandia Mountains

The people of Albuquerque are fortunate to have the the Sandia Mountains so close to home. The area provides both advanced routes for the experienced skier as well as intermediate and beginner areas, replete with beautiful scenery and views. The following trails are divided into sections of beginner, intermediate, and advanced, for better ski-tour planning. They are all found on the east side of the Sandias, accessed off New Mexico 536, which heads into Cibola National Forest from New Mexico North 14 at Antonito and Sandia Park. NM 536 is always plowed to the Sandia Peak Ski Basin, but it sometimes takes a day or two for the road to be cleared to Sandia Crest. Check with Sandia Ranger Station or the sheriff's office for road information.

Sandia Mountains—Class I

CIENEGA PICNIC GROUND ROAD:
Class I   3 miles   Elevation: 7,200-7,500 feet

When snow conditions permit, beginners can ski this easy access road into Cienega Picnic Ground. The entrance to the picnic ground lies just past the Cibola National Forest boundary on NM 536, 2 miles west of the junction of NM 14 at Antonito. You can leave your car below the locked gate, and ski south up the forest road to the stop sign. Turn west (right) and follow the easy route into the picnic ground. The road terminates at the Cienega Canyon trailhead.

SULPHUR CANYON ROAD:
Class I   1 1/2 miles   Elevation: 7,200-7,600 feet

Sulphur Canyon Road is accessed off the road to Cienega Picnic Ground, 2 miles west of NM 14 on NM 536. Instead of following the road south into Cienega, turn north (right) and follow the moderately steep road through the picnic ground into an old summer home area. The road terminates at Faulty Trail, which the more advanced skier can follow north or south, if conditions permit.

LAS HUERTAS CANYON ROAD:
Class I   5 miles   Elevation: 8,600-7,900 feet

The upper portion of Las Huertas Road, which travels through Las Huertas Canyon from NM 536 to Placitas, provides good skiing because of its elevation and inaccessibility to cars (the road is supposedly closed to motor vehicles in the winter, but vehicular traffic is common, especially on the lower portion near Placitas). Leave your car at Balsam Glade Picnic Ground and follow the windy road several miles down to the Cooper-Ellis Ranch in Capulin Canyon. The views north to the Sangre de Cristos are spectacular, and the downhill run is effortless, but be sure to save some energy for the uphill climb back to your car. Another route utilizing the upper portion of the road is described in the Capulin-Challenge Trail route, and if conditions permit, stronger skiers can arrange for transportation and ski the entire Las Huertas Road to the northern Cibola Forest Boundary at Placitas (you have to get out there during, or immediately after, a snow storm, or you'll run into cars and poor snow conditions).

Sandia Mountains—Class II

TRAMWAY SERVICE ROAD:
Class I-II   2 miles   Elevation: 10,300 feet

Perhaps the most popular area in the Sandias, the Tramway Service Road provides good conditions for beginners along the first part of the route, and more advanced terrain for experienced skiers near the Tram terminal. Skiers can also enjoy the warmth and comfort of the restaurant at the Tramway. The road lies on NM 536, the Crest Highway, 4.7 miles west of the junction with

NM 165. You'll know you're there when you see the line of cars parked alongside the highway.

The first part of the road is a gradual ascent south to the gate, where Challenge Trail turns off to the east (left) and Switchback Trail and trails to Kiwanis Meadow head west (right). The service road levels out as it passes by the gravel pit, where occasionally you'll see telemark skiers zooming down the steep slope above the pit from Gravel Pit Trail. Beginners probably will want to stop just beyond the gravel pit, where the service road descends its first hill, levels out, then descends again in a long glide to the Tramway. More experienced skiers can return to NM 536 along several alternate routes, described later: Gravel Pit Trail to Survey Trail, or Crest Trail to Survey Trail. If you return along the service road, be careful to ski along the right-hand side of the road to avoid the other skiers (especially the skaters) zooming down the hills.

KIWANIS MEADOW ROUTE—GRAVEL PIT TRAIL:
Class II   2 miles   Elevation: 10,400-10,300 feet

This system of trails is an alternate route for intermediate skiers to reach the Tramway, avoiding the busy Tram Service Road. Take NM 536 to Sandia Crest (6 miles west of the junction with NM 165) and park in the lower parking lot (usually the only one plowed). Kiwanis Meadow Route begins in the lower southeast corner of the parking area, signified by a Forest Service gate. The ski trail, an old access road, is an easy glide down to Kiwanis Meadow, where the Crest Trail descends from Kiwanis Cabin south to the Tramway. Views from the cabin look west to Albuquerque and south over Cañon de Domingo Baca to the Tram. Conditions in the meadow vary from excellent telemark powder to treacherous crust and ice.

Ski south across the meadow to the southeast corner, where Gravel Pit Trail heads south, into the trees (another blazed trail begins just to the east of Gravel Pit Trail and leads directly down to the service road). Just a few yards beyond the meadow the trail emerges from the trees above the gravel pit, where you can see the skiers below on the Tram Service Road, and north to the Sangre de Cristo Mountains above Santa Fe. The trail reenters the trees and follows a narrow, downhill path to the Tram. Gravel Pit Trail provides an easier route to the Tram than the steeper Crest Trail above it (you can see and hear skiers on that trail). The two trails merge just before the Tram, and terminate at the top of the downhill ski area at the south end of the Tramway Service Road. There are several alternate routes back to the Crest: along the Tram Service Road to Survey Trail and Kiwanis Meadow, or along Crest Trail to the meadow. It's all uphill coming back, so don't indulge yourself too much at the restaurant.

CAPULIN TRAIL—CHALLENGE TRAIL:
Class II   3½ miles   Elevation: 8,900 feet

This loop around Capulin Picnic Ground to Challenge Trail is a a good alternative to ski when the Crest Highway hasn't been plowed. Capulin Picnic Ground is located on New Mexico 536 about ¼-mile west of the junction of New Mexico 165, where 165 descends on the 8-mile dirt road to Placitas. Drive into the picnic ground (usually plowed) to the north end of the parking lot. The trailhead is marked with blue cross-country diamonds.

Capulin Trail heads north a short distance, then turns west (left) and starts to loop around the west side of the snow-play area. Watch for trail markers as it turns south after a short but steep climb. Another short climb brings you to a downhill glide as the trail passes through Capulin Canyon (underneath the power line) and back south to the Crest Highway.

Cross the highway to the trail blazes pointing southwest—this is the old road (before the reconstruction of the Crest Highway switchbacks) leading to Nine Mile Picnic Ground. Turn left onto the new road into the picnic area; if it's been plowed you'll have to ski along the piled-up banks. Nine Mile is a good place to stop and rest or eat, if you can find the picnic tables beneath the snow.

To continue the loop, ski southwest along the picnic ground

road until you come to the outhouse. Look to your left, up in the trees, and you'll see the blue blazes marking the spur trail which connects to Challenge Trail, your destination. It's about a half-mile climb up through the trees to the stand of fir trees where you'll find Challenge Trail coming down the mountain from the Tram Service Road. Your route continues east (left), down the mountain on Challenge Trail.

It's all downhill from here. The first glide through the trees is fairly benign, but there is a steep pitch a little later on where you might find yourself negotiating the trail in a sitting position. Follow the trail blazes closely where the trail temporarily levels out across an open area. It again enters the trees to the east; begin to watch for sections of the Crest Highway to appear to the left. Just before the trail starts to climb a ridge to the right, leave the trail and ski down a short distance to the highway. You will come out just below the entrance to Capulin Picnic Ground, so ski back up the side of the highway and back into the picnic area.

You might want to ski another fun downhill slope leading east, out of Capulin Picnic Ground, down to Las Huertas Road (you'll then have to climb back up to your car or catch a ride). The trail begins just south of the outhouse in the lower parking lot. It's a fairly gentle glide down to the lower Capulin Road (at the iron gate), which in turn leads down a wide trail to Las Huertas Road (the continuation of NM 165 to Placitas), just below Balsam Glade Picnic Ground. We once took my husband's cousin, from New York, down this run on her very first day of cross-country skiing. While I can't say she didn't spend some time lying in the snow, it was enough fun for her to whet her appetite for more. In fact, she turned into a hot dog telemark skier up in the White Mountains of New Hampshire.

At Las Huertas Road, turn to the right, and a short uphill climb brings you to the junction with the Crest Highway. The Capulin-Challenge route is not measured for distance, but my best guess is that it's only a 3-3$^{1}/_{2}$-mile trip. Add another 1$^{1}/_{2}$ miles if you intend to ski down to Las Huertas Road.

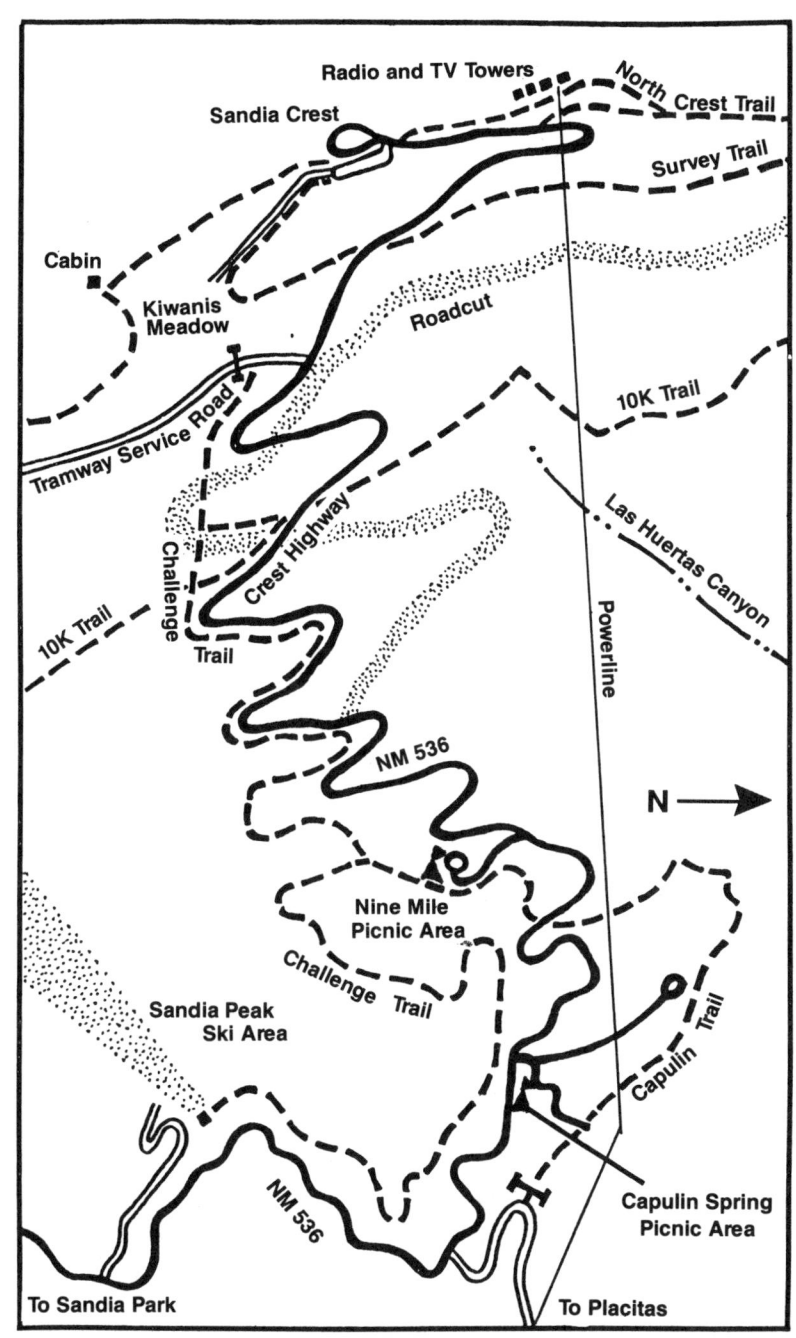

CAPULIN TRAIL—CHALLENGE TRAIL

BURIED CABLE TRAIL—SWITCHBACK TRAIL:
Class II   3 miles   Elevation: 10,400 feet

Buried Cable Trail and Switchback Trail make a nice intermediate loop in the trees north of Kiwanis Meadow. To find the trailhead, park in the Crest parking lot on NM 536 and follow Kiwanis Meadow Route south to Kiwanis Meadow. As you emerge from the trees, ski east down the open slope of the meadow. Head north, back into the trees, where Buried Cable Trail heads northwest, back towards NM 536. Follow the arrow on the tree to the left (the arrow to the right indicates Switchback Trail). It's an uphill climb to the junction with Switchback Trail, which originates on the Kiwanis Meadow Route (to the left). Bear right and follow Switchback Trail north as it levels out before making its switchback south, just before the Crest Highway. The return route is a fun downhill glide through the trees back to the junction with Buried Cable Trail.

Sandia Mountains—Class III

SOUTH CREST TRAIL to TRAMWAY:
Class III   3 miles   Elevation: 10,600-10,300 feet

While this trail follows the ridgeline of the Sandias and affords magnificent views west over Albuquerque, conditions are sometimes poor due to wind and exposure. The trailhead is on NM 536 at Sandia Crest, 6 miles west of the junction with NM 165.

The trail heads south from the parking lot; follow the lower route into the trees along the interpretive trail to Kiwanis Cabin above Kiwanis Meadow. From the cabin the trail descends east along the ridgeline, then turns south again in a steep descent into the trees (above Gravel Pit Trail). This section of the trail has many steep pitches and can be quite treacherous if snow conditions are icy. Just before the Tramway it ties in with Gravel Pit Trail. You can ski back to the parking lot on Gravel Pit Trail to Kiwanis Meadow Route, or Tramway Service Road to Survey Trail and Kiwanis Meadow Route.

KIWANIS MEADOW ROUTE—SURVEY TRAIL—10K TRAIL—NORTH CREST TRAIL:
Class III   6 miles   Elevation: 10,000 feet

This loop is for the cross country skier with lots of stamina and good downhill skills. It both begins and ends at the Sandia Crest parking lot, although you may choose from several alternate routes back, ending at other return points.

Tale NM 536 to Sandia Crest (6 miles west of the junction with NM 165) and park in the lower lot. Kiwanis Meadow Route begins in the lower southeast corner of the Crest parking area, signified by a Forest Service gate. The ski trail, an old access road, is an easy glide down to Kiwanis Meadow, where the Crest Trail descends from Kiwanis Cabin south to the Tramway. Views from the cabin look west to Albuquerque and south over Cañon de Domingo Baca to the Tram. Snow conditions in the meadow vary from excellent telemark powder to treacherous crust and ice.

Instead of skiing south across the meadow to the Crest Trail, ski east down the open slope of the meadow where you emerge from the road. Just to the north, several blazed trails (blue diamonds) enter the trees. Buried Cable Trail leads left, back to the Crest parking lot or in a loop with Switchback Trail. Stay to the right and follow the blazes in a northeasterly direction. There are several spur trails along this route, but they all merge as you continue north toward the Crest Highway. A short spur trail to the right leads down to the Tramway Service Road, a favorite beginner area.

Just south of the Crest Highway, Survey Trail turns west and parallels the highway across several openings and back into the trees again. It finally emerges at the highway, which you must cross to the north side to continue the tour.

The northern part of Survey Trail is considerably more difficult than the part just described. The trail traverses north toward Cañon Media in narrow, steep swoops through the trees. Keep an eye out for the trail blazes, but be careful not to wrap around a tree as the trail zig-zags around bends. There are several steep ascents and descents along the first part of the 1.6 miles to the junction of 10K Trail. The second half is mostly moderate, with wonderful downhill glides.

At the junction of 10K Trail there are several alternate routes back to the Crest Highway (Survey Trail was recently extended north from 10K Trail and ties in with North Crest Trail). To the east (right), 10K descends about $1/4$ mile to one of the roadcuts which traverse this northeast side of the Sandias. These cuts were blazed back in the early 1970s for a proposed rerouting of the Crest Highway to Placitas. The plan died under a barrage of criticism against such a high-impact use of the mountains, but these initial roadcuts remain. You can follow this roadcut south (right) back to the Crest Highway, or continue east on 10K, back into the trees (it's blazed) and follow the $2^{1}/2$-mile trail back to the highway (the trail and roadcut basically parallel one another). This trail is quite difficult, however, replete with precipitous descents through narrow swaths of trees and long, uphill climbs. 10K Trail comes out $2^{1}/3$ miles below the Crest on the highway.

My preferred route back to the Crest is North Crest Trail. At the junction of Survey Trail and 10K, turn west (left) and climb the short distance to the Cañnon del Agua Overlook on North Crest Trail (if snow conditions are bad you might want to hike this steep climb rather than ski it). At the overlook views stretch across the Rio Grande to Mount Taylor, Cabezon, and the Jemez Mountains. North Peak, covered with aspens, is just to your left, south of the overlook. This is the backside of the big rock face called the Shield that you see from Albuquerque. From the overlook, North Crest Trail continues north 9 more miles down the mountains to Tunnel Spring, near Placitas.

The route back to the Crest is 2 miles south (left) on North Crest Trail, along the rim of the Sandias. The trail enters the aspen trees at the south end of the overlook clearing, and follows fairly easy uphill terrain. All along the trail views open up on the ridge above the precipitous west face of the mountains. You'll pass the Needle, Prow, del Agua Spire, and various other famous rock

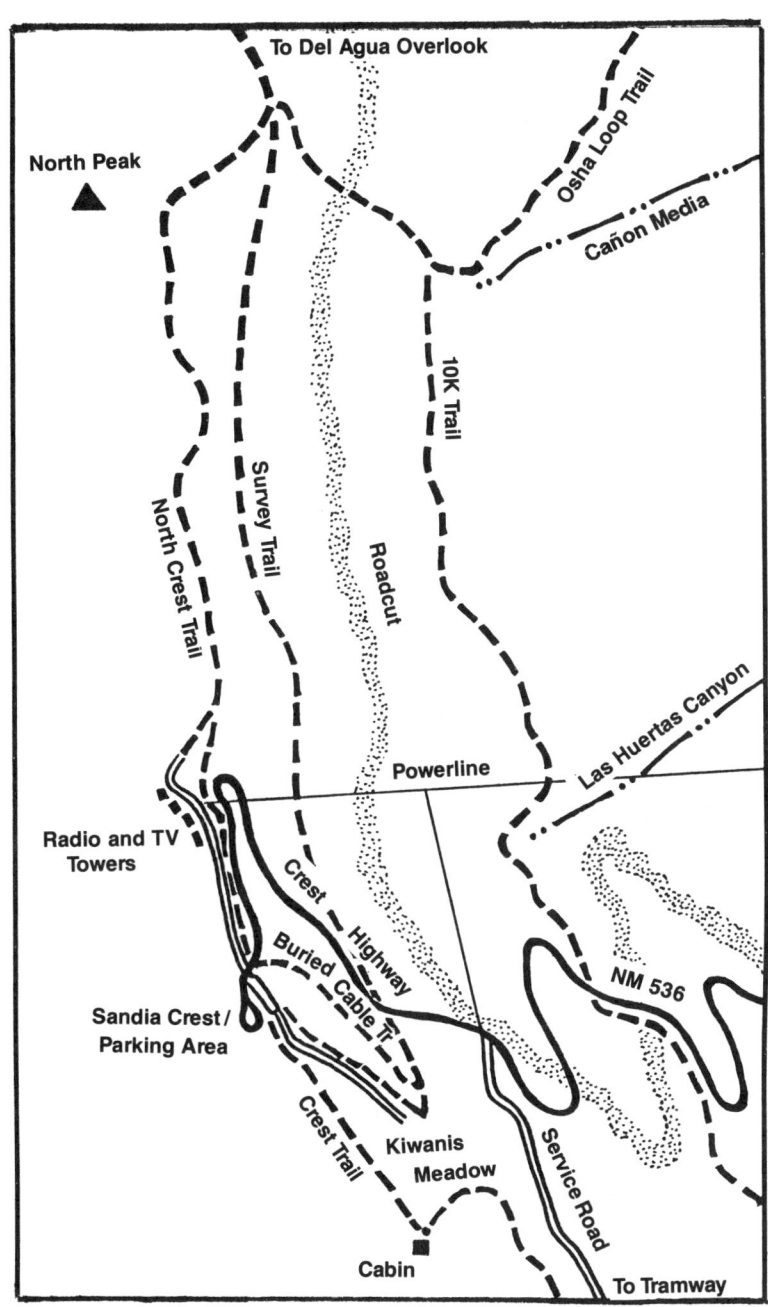

SANDIA CREST AREA

climbs.

The trail becomes steeper above Chimney Canyon, still basically following the ridgeline south. By the last half mile, you're looking for the electronic site towers signifying journey's end. Luckily, this last half mile is an easy glide across the mountains below the electronic site road. The trail emerges just across the highway from the Crest parking lot. The entire route is approximately 6 miles, and quite rigorous.

10K TRAIL:
Class III   5-10 miles   Elevation: 10,000 feet

You can ski north or south from NM 536 on 10K Trail, although both routes are quite rigorous. The trailhead for both lies on NM 536, 3.7 miles west of the junction with NM 165, at the roadcut. Parking can sometimes be a problem, unless the snowplows have created parking pull-offs alongside the road.

North 10K Trail follows blue blazes that begin just above the roadcut and follow the up and down terrain across Las Huertas Canyon to Cañon Media, where a spur trail leads east to Media Spring. From here it's a steep ascent to another roadcut, which leads north all the way to the ridgeline of the Sandias, and south back to NM 536. Across the roadcut, 10K Trail continues uphill to the junction with Survey Trail, and on to Del Agua Overlook on North Crest Trail. North 10K Trail can be skied in conjunction with Survey Trail or North Crest Trail as a loop route for the experienced skier.

South 10K Trail begins at the roadcut on the south side of the highway, heads east into the trees, paralleling the highway, then turns south, into the trees. It traverses a canyon for about $3/4$ mile until it meets the first of the Sandia Peak downhill ski slopes. Follow the blue blazes on the trees as it crosses eight slopes (watch out for downhill skiers), then descends steeply into Cañon Madera before leveling out at the junction with Tree Spring Trail and South Crest Trail.

CHALLENGE TRAIL:
Class III   4½ miles   Elevation: 10,000-8,500 feet

This is a cross-country trail for those skiers who remain downhillers at heart. It's a 4½-mile descent of the Sandias from the Tramway Service Road to the base of the Sandia Peak Ski Basin, with many steep pitches and narrow runs along the way.

There are several ways to approach this adventure. If you drive to the Tram Service Road along New Mexico 536, the Crest Highway, and ski down the trail, you will have to arrange to be picked up at the ski basin and returned to your car. An alternative is to park at the ski area, buy a one-way ticket on the chairlift, ski along the service road to the trail, then down to your car. I recommend this approach to facilitate transportation—a one-way ticket is not too expensive, and an occasional indulgence is fun.

Challenge Trail is right next to the iron gate at the beginning of the Tram Service Road off New Mexico 536. It's designated most difficult and is blazed the entire way with the standard blue cross-country diamonds.

The trail basically parallels the Crest Highway, in the cover of the spruce-fir vegetation, until it crosses the first roadcut (the blaze for the rerouting of the Crest Highway described in the previous section). The blue diamonds guide you across the roadcut through an island of trees, then onto a second roadcut doubling back to the north. Follow this part of the roadcut north, toward the highway, until you see the blue diamonds directing you back into the trees. This part of the trail carries you down to the junction with the 10K Trail, marked advanced, which heads south toward the ski basin.

Challenge Trail continues downhill from 10K Trail, and winds in and out of the trees along the highway to the first junction with a half-mile trail leading north to Nine Mile Picnic Ground. The trail is very near the highway here, and passes through a large open area full of prickly locust bushes. Stay to the right and follow Challenge Trail around in a loop as it circles back to the north and again joins with a spur trail to the picnic ground. Just beyond this junction, Challenge Trail veers off to the east, downhill, where it meets another spur trail from the picnic ground. Stay to the right, and Challenge Trail swoops down through the trees, crosses an open area, and descends in a steep pitch to a spur trail which leads out to the Crest Highway near Capulin Picnic Ground. Stay to the right, following the blue blazes, and the trail levels out as it nears the Crest Highway-New Mexico 165 junction. The trail then turns south (right), paralleling NM 536 (the road is not visible from the trail), and picks up an old ski basin road which it follows down to the poma lift at the north end of the ski area.

It's best to ski Challenge Trail after a fresh snow, as conditions deteriorate rapidly on the lower portion of the trail.

NORTH CREST TRAIL to TUNNEL SPRING:
Class III   11 miles   Elevation: 10,600-6,200 feet

If snow conditions permit, you can ski the entire 11 miles of the North Crest Trail from Sandia Crest to Tunnel Spring on the north end of the Sandias near Placitas. The trail conforms, except for the first 2 miles to Del Agua Overlook, to the standard Forest Service 8% grade, and is only moderately steep.

North Crest Trail begins on the north side of NM 536 at Sandia Crest. The first half mile is an easy glide just below the power lines. Once the trail reaches the rim of the mountains the terrain becomes steeper and provides some exhilarating swoops down through the trees, interspersed with great views. As the trail emerges at Del Agua Overlook, 10K Trail heads east, down through the trees towards Survey Trail and the roadcut. North Crest Trail continues north to a second overlook, then heads back into the trees as it leaves the rim of the mountains. Here the trail is much less steep than the previous 2 miles. It junctions with Osha Loop Trail at about $2^1/_2$ miles and the upper roadcut at the north Del Agua Overlook at about 3 miles. The trail again leaves the rim here and begins the switchbacks down the east side of the mountains through the low-growing gambel oak. Views extend north to the Sangre de Cristos and east to the Jemez Mountains. Just before the trail enters the piñon-juniper vegetation of the lower elevations, at the limestone ledge, Peñasco Blanco Trail heads south across the mountains to Cañon Osha. North Crest Trail continues northeast, following the rim of Cañon Agua Sarca, where a stone bench provides respite and a view north over the Placitas area to the Jemez.

From here to the trailhead at Tunnel Spring the snow may not be good enough to ski unless it's an exceptional snow year. Watch for the turn more directly north as the trail swings over towards Placitas; various old mining routes lead east, down to Dome Valley. The trail then veers west for 2 miles to Tunnel Spring.

CIBOLA NATIONAL FOREST

San Mateo Mountains—Mount Taylor

The Mount Taylor area of Cibola National Forest affords some of the most remote and spectacular ski touring in New Mexico, and if you ski to Mount Taylor itself—the powerful sacred mountain of both the Pueblo and Navajo Indians—you will indeed feel like you have arrived at the center of the universe.

LA MOSCA CANYON ROAD:
Class II   12 miles   Elevation: 9,000-11,000 feet

Take New Mexico 547, Lobo Canyon Road, north out of Grants. New Mexico 547 becomes Forest Road 239 past the turnoff to Lobo Canyon Campground. At mile 17 is the intersection of Forest Road 453 which leads 6 miles to La Mosca Lookout and Mount Taylor. FR 239 is usually not plowed beyond the pavement and FR 453 is only plowed just before the quadrathalon event held in the area in February, but you can usually make it to the intersection of the two roads (with snow tires, chains, or four-wheel drive) to begin your tour.

Forest Road 453 crosses a ridge for several miles along fairly level terrain. At Rock Spring, before you head into La Mosca Canyon, the Forest Service has blazed several cross-country trails heading south to El Rito Canyon and Mount Taylor. The lower trail (to the right) heads three-fourths of a mile to El Rito Canyon and is geared to the beginner. In El Rito Canyon, a trail marked most difficult leads south to Cienega Spring; this was intended to circle around to the north and return to El Rito Canyon near Rock Tank, but has yet to be blazed. Another trail, designated more difficult, turns east just past Cienega Spring (uphill) and continues to Twin Spring, where an expert loop has been planned around the Mirabel Spring area (to my knowledge this has yet to be blazed as well).

Back on FR 453, the upper trail (to the left), marked more difficult, is a steady climb of several miles over to the exposed slopes of Mount Taylor. It enters El Rito Canyon, crosses the open snowfields on the northwest side of Taylor, and then climbs through thick spruce-fir forest to the exposed southwest slopes of the mountain, affording panoramic views. From here it's a straight shot up along the treeline to the top of Taylor. You can also pick up the Mount Taylor clearcut logging road (described a little further on) just below the summit and follow this road back to FR 453.

Past Rock Spring, FR 453 enters La Mosca Canyon in its ascent toward Mount Taylor. Several years ago the Forest Service blazed a new logging road through the canyon, bypassing the original La Mosca Canyon road which follows the canyon bottom. The new road crosses the canyon to the north side and climbs along the ridge to a series of switchbacks. The Forest Service recommends that skiers use the old road to the switchbacks and snowmobilers use the new road to avoid conflicts.

Both sections of the road intersect at the switchbacks up the north side (a logging access road takes off to the west and is closed off by a gate; stay to the east (right) on the ski route). As you emerge from the aspen trees just below La Mosca Peak you can

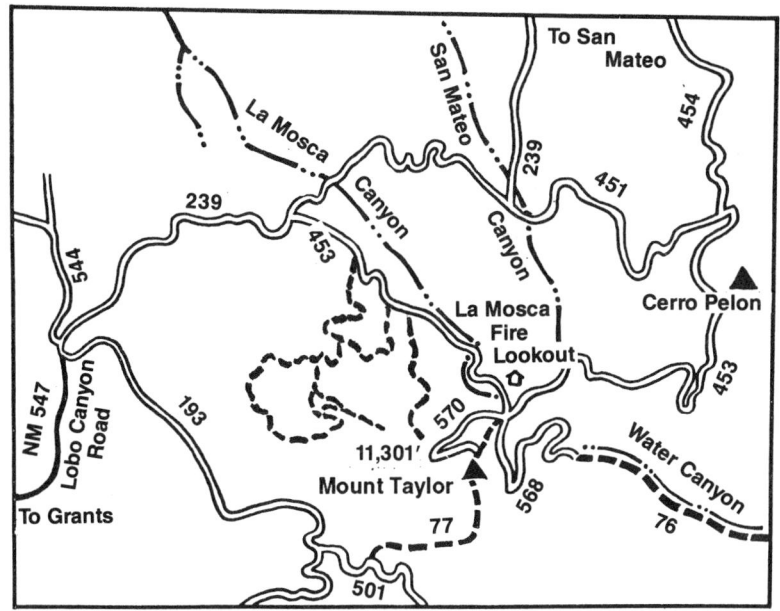

MOUNT TAYLOR AREA: LA MOSCA CANYON; SAN MATEO CANYON

see the precariously perched fire lookout and electronic site. The road turns south here, at the base of La Mosca Peak, and continues toward the saddle between Mount Taylor and La Mosca.

At the saddle there is a three-way junction: to the northeast, FR 453 continues across the exposed slope of La Mosca Peak to the fire lookout; to the south, downhill, a road leads into Water Canyon and dead ends at a trail leading to the forest boundary; to the southwest, an old logging road leads through the Mount Taylor clearcut around to the west side of the mountain. You can ski any of the road routes. Forest Road 453 continues past La Mosca Fire Lookout, makes a loop around the east end of the district, and eventually leads back to Lobo Canyon Road. Water Canyon is a beautiful, narrow canyon which descends east toward the Laguna Indian Pueblo and contains one of the few live streams in the Mount Taylor district. You can make a loop trail by skiing along the Mount Taylor logging road (it's a steep ascent) to a connecting expert route that leads through the trees back to FR 453 at the bottom of La Mosca Canyon. If you stop at the saddle, your round-trip along FR 453 is 12 miles.

SAN MATEO CANYON ROAD:
Class II-III   Elevation: 9,000-10,000 feet

The San Mateo Canyon area, the continuation of Forest Road 239, provides excellent ski touring for the more experienced skier who wants to travel through the beautiful north side canyons of Mount Taylor. Access can be a problem, however, as FR 239 is usually unmaintained past the paving or the turnoff to La Mosca Canyon unless it is being used by a logging company as access to a site. Before planning a trip to the area, call the Mount Taylor Ranger Station in Grants to find out about road conditions. If the road has not been plowed you can sometimes make it to the San Mateo area with chains or four-wheel drive.

Take FR 239 past the La Mosca turnoff (Forest Road 453), 5 more miles to where FR 239 turns sharply east and narrows considerably as it starts its climb toward San Mateo Spring. From here you can ski as far as you like along FR 239; the road climbs through Salazar Canyon and San Mateo Canyon to an area called Spud Patch beneath rock walls. Here the road levels out for awhile, then climbs to American Canyon and on to the junction with FR 453 coming north from La Mosca Peak. We once drove as far as Spud Patch, skied to the junction with 453, made a campfire, and spent the rest of the day playing around in the aspen meadows and taking in the views east over the Rio Puerco to the Sandias. Snow conditions along this road are almost always good because of its northern exposure, but you must be careful of snowmobilers who also use the road.

CIBOLA NATIONAL FOREST

Zuni Mountains

McGAFFEY LAKE

The McGaffey Lake area is one of the few areas in the Zuni mountains accessible in the wintertime, and consequently used by cross-country skiers. Forest Road 400 leads south from U.S. 66 (about 12 miles east of Gallup) to Fort Wingate. From Fort Wingate the road is maintained to the McGaffey Lake and summer home area, where other forest roads lead farther south into the Zuni Mountains. Skiers can follow Forest Road 50 toward McGaffey Lookout and enjoy the open terrain south of the lake in a $3^1/_2$-mile radius. This area is particularly good for spring skiing, but can be quite windy in the winter.

CIBOLA NATIONAL FOREST

Manzano Mountains

There are several areas in the Manzano that are suitable for skiing with sufficient snowfall. A newly developed commercial ski track in the Albuquerque Trail area was developed in 1993. All the ski trails are located on the east side of the mountains, accessible from South New Mexico 337 (formerly South 14).

FOREST ROAD 55 from TAJIQUE to FOURTH OF JULY CAMPGROUND:

As of 1993, Forest Road 55 out of Tajique (31 miles south of I-40 on NM 337) is plowed to the commercial ski track at Albuquerque Trailhead, opening up the rest of the area to good ski touring. It's only a short distance from Albuquerque Trail to Fourth of July Campground, and you can ski into the campground to Fourth of July Trail. You can also ski along FR 55 toward Torreon, using some of the old logging roads that detour off the main road. The trails which intersect FR 55—Fourth of July, Cerro Blanco, Bosque, and Trail Canyon—are really too steep for good cross-country skiing, although the experienced ski tourer can use them for access to the Manzano Crest Trail. Several of these trails were recently gated to prevent off-road vehicle use.

RED CANYON CAMPGROUND:

Forest Road 253 out of the town of Manzano to Red Canyon Campground is not maintained during the winter, but if you can get close to the campground, the series of logging roads off Forest Road 422 provide some good cross-country skiing. Manzano lies 39 miles south of I-40 on NM 337; FR 253 heads west 6 miles to Red Canyon Campground.

Forest Road 422 leads south from FR 253, 4 miles west of Manzano. Ski up this road 2 miles to the directional sign for Ox Canyon Trail to the northwest (right). Follow this road to the "Primitive Road" sign and turn right, instead of left to the trailhead. This road will take you in a loop back to FR 253. If you turn left, toward the trailhead, it's an easy cross-country tour to the junction with a logging road turning south. This logging road eventually leads back to FR 422, and you can ski back (north) along FR 422 to FR 253.

Beyond these loops, FR 422 continues several miles south to the junction with Forest Road 275, (recently gated to prevent off-road vehicle use) which leads to Kayser Mill Trail and provides additional skiing routes along connecting logging roads. This is a long way from FR 253, however, and requires more than a day's ski-touring time.

Opposite Page:

MANZANO MOUNTAINS: FOURTH OF JULY;
NEW CANYON—CAPILLA PEAK; RED CANYON

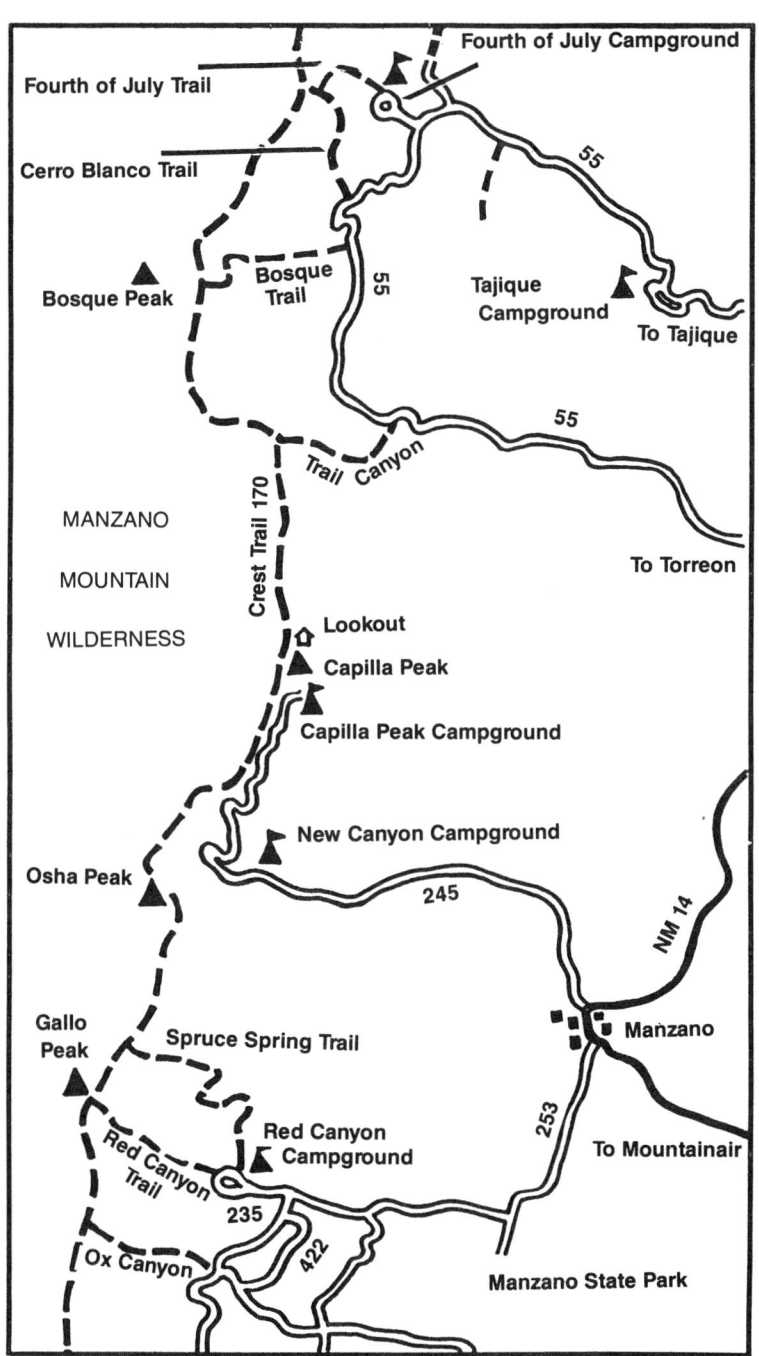

NEW CANYON—FOREST ROAD 245:

Forest Road 245 out of Manzano to New Canyon Campground and Capilla Peak is also not maintained during the winter except for occasional service vehicles. It's 9 miles to Capilla Peak where you can ski along the loop road in Capilla Peak Campground (the last 4 miles are quite steep). The Manzano Crest Trail heads south here to Osha Peak, and can be skied, though there are precipitous sections and rugged climbs. The Crest Trail north to Comanche Canyon and Trail Canyon is too steep for good ski touring. If there is too much snow to make it all the way to Capilla Peak, you can ski the several miles to New Canyon Campground and follow an old logging road north for a shorter ski tour.

SANTA FE NATIONAL FOREST

Jemez Mountains

Less steep and at a lower elevation than most of the other mountain ranges in New Mexico, the Jemez Mountains offer good beginner and intermediate terrain but conditions that deteriorate rapidly. Over the years, the Jemez has been heavily logged and many of the ski trails described follow old logging roads, which contributes to its reputation as a beginner area. An ancient volcano created the huge caldera—Valle Grande—that is the centerpiece of the Jemez, with many of the ski trails following the ridgelines, affording views across its open, valley terrain. The San Pedro Parks Wilderness area, on the north side of the Jemez Mountains, provides more opportunity for the experienced skier, and is less utilized than those routes accessed off NM 4.

If you're driving to the Jemez from Albuquerque, take the New Mexico 44 exit west off of I-25 and drive through Bernalillo to the junction with New Mexico 4 at San Ysidro (25 miles). Follow NM 4 through Jemez Pueblo and Jemez Springs to the junction of NM 4 and NM 126. Several ski trails are accessed to the west, along NM 126, and many more east along NM 4. If you're coming from northern New Mexico, take NM 502 west from Pojoaque to NM 4, which leads through Bandelier National Monument to the St. Peter's Dome area.

To access San Pedro Parks Wilderness, take NM 44 west out of Bernalillo to San Ysidro, and continue on NM 44 to the town of Cuba. NM 126 leads east to the Parks.

Jemez Mountains—NM 126 Area

SAN ANTONIO HOT SPRING:
Class II   8 miles   Elevation: 7,700-8,000 feet
   There are two routes into San Antonio Hot Spring: Forest Road

132 to a connecting trail on the east side of San Antonio Creek; and Forest Road 376, 5 miles in along the west side of the creek. I prefer the former, the road-trail combination, as there is more diversity and elevation change, and consequently more adventurous skiing. It's shorter in length, at 4 miles, but more difficult due to the nature of the terrain.

Drive 1.9 miles on New Mexico 126 from La Cueva junction (NM 126 turns west—left—toward Fenton Lake; New Mexico 4 turns east—right—toward Los Alamos). There is room to park where FR 132 turns north off NM 126. The first half mile or so of the forest road is access to private land, and you'll sometimes have to contend with tire ruts and melting conditions. Once past the private land, however, the traffic clears and as the road follows San Antonio Creek north it's a beautiful $1^1/_2$-mile route along moderately hilly terrain to the trailhead. There are numerous resting areas alongside the creek tempting you to slow down and enjoy this winter riparian scene. If the hot spring is your destination, however, there's not that much time to linger on your 8-mile round trip.

At the end of the road the trail ascends a steep hill, continuing north. At the top of this first short hill two routes diverge: to the right, the trail climbs another hill to the upper trail along a fairly level route; to the left, the trail swoops downhill to follow the creek. The trails converge a mile farther on. The route closer to the creek is more scenic, but more difficult, especially in the meadow where you must climb a steep hill (this may mean sidestep) to the junction with the upper trail. The upper trail passes through stands of aspen to the meadow in an easier route. The meadow provides some good hills for telemark practice; save your practice session for the return trip so you don't have to climb back up the trail to continue your journey.

On the north side of the meadow where the trails converge, a stream has usually melted the snow and you must remove your skis and walk up a short hill to where the trail is once again snow-covered. Several hills later another stream along a fenceline crosses the trail and you must again remove your skis to cross. Here the canyon narrows and you ski along the high east ridge of the creek. The multicolored sheer rock canyon walls rise to the west where FR 376 makes its descent to the hot spring. The canyon opens up where the trail and 376 converge at the spring. The trail emerges just south of several Forest Service buildings inside the wooden fence compound. Climb over the fence (almost buried in snow) and continue along the east side of the buildings to the steep hiking trail up the hill (east) to the spring. Forest Road 376 comes down to a parking area north of the spring and a short trail leads south to the buildings.

There is no better antidote to cold hands and feet and tired muscles than the San Antonio Hot Spring. Take a bath first, then eat lunch once you are warm and relaxed. Please leave the spring as you found it, clean and inviting.

The return trip along the trail is mostly downhill, luckily, after your muscles have been jellied by 101° temperatures. If you choose to return by FR 376, ski to the parking lot and up the road out of the canyon. The road then levels out along the 5-mile return trip, and comes out on NM 126 about 2 miles west of FR 132.

Jemez Mountains—Redondo Campground

REDONDO CAMPGROUND:
Class I-II 2-4 miles Elevation: 8,100 feet

A favorite beginner's cross-country area, both because of terrain and access, Redondo Campground offers good skiing for the more experienced skier too.

At the junction of NM 126 (west to Fenton Lake) and NM 4, take 4 east (right) for 2.2 miles to Redondo Campground. There is a large Forest Service sign on the north side of the highway marking the campground. Continue about 100 feet farther along the highway to a pull-off on the south, at the Jemez Canyon Overlook. Ski trails also take off on the overlook side of the road leading out

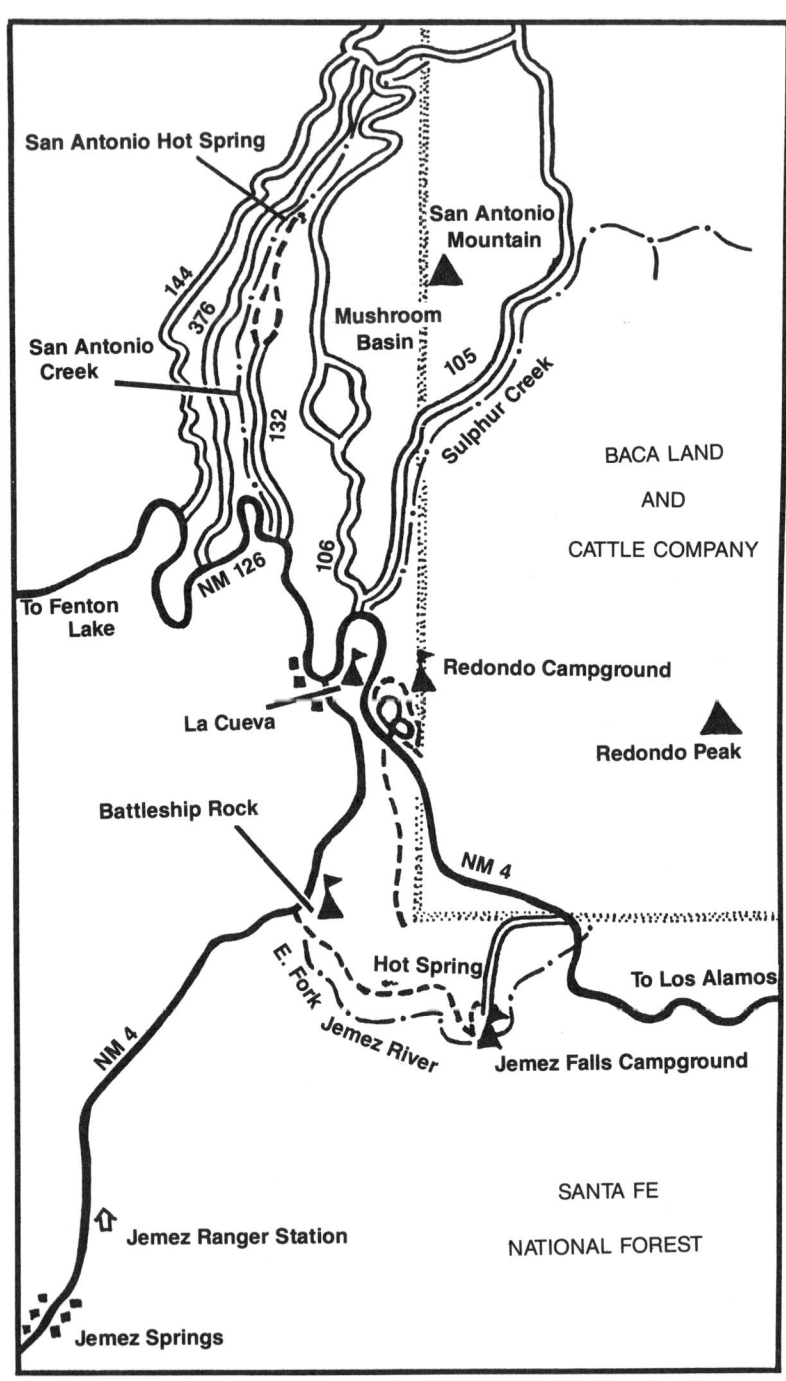

to the vista and along an old logging road.

Directly across the highway is a trail leading into the campground. Put on your skis and ski the hundred or so yards to the main campground road. There is a sign to your left which shows the layout of the three loops comprising the campground. If you are a beginner and wish to practice on some wide, easy terrain, the loops are a good place to begin. They all circle back to the point of origin at the sign.

To find the blazed cross-country ski trails extending out from the campground, ski to the east (right) from the sign along the main campground road. You'll enter the second loop at a gate, and when you come to the outhouse, look to the right and you'll see the blue diamonds marking a trail to the south (right). Follow the clearly defined trail that leads back toward NM 4 in a few up-and-down hills. As the highway becomes visible the trail turns east (left), up the hill, to a junction marked with arrows on a tree. The trail to the left, called Redondo Loop by the New Mexico Ski Touring Club, is the easier trail, heading north again in a wide circle around the campground. The intermediate trail continues up the hill, basically following NM 4 to the Valle Grande fenceline. This trail is named Crater Spur Trail and has some steeper hills to negotiate.

CRATER SPUR TRAIL:
1 mile

At the junction of these two trails, continue east up through the trees along this intermediate trail. Watch for the blue blazes as the trail crosses the crater in the direction of NM 4. When you can once again see the highway, stay to the left and follow the trail back to the trees. A little farther on, the trail meets the Valle

Opposite Page:

LA CUEVA AREA: SAN ANTONIO HOT SPRING; REDONDO CAMPGROUND

Grande fence, private land closed to skiers. Here another blazed route follows a logging road which leads in a circle back to the original trail in the large bowl. Ski back to the campground the same way you came.

REDONDO LOOP TRAIL:
2 1/2 miles

This beginner trail makes a wide loop around Redondo Campground and emerges at the west end of the main campground road. You can follow it either way, but I prefer to start out to the east, at the junction of the Crater Spur Trail.

At this junction follow the arrows north along a fairly level route through the trees. You're on the east side of the campground, and if you look to the north you can catch glimpses of the snow-covered Redondo Peak. The trail goes due north to a junction of some ski tracks veering off down through a bowl to the left. The main trail continues straight ahead, through a narrow swath of trees, then begins to turn toward the west. There are some nice glides through the trees as the Valle Grande fenceline comes into view. The trail continues northwest through some open areas along the fenceline. You may come across a patch of snow obviously trampled and packed down—an elk bedding area.

The trail now heads south around the west end of the campground. The terrain is a little hilly here, with some climbs and downhill glides. You're skiing back toward the highway, and right at the edge of the road the trail turns sharply left and climbs a short hill to an old road leading to the campground. Beginners often have to resort to a sidestep to negotiate this hill, especially if the snow is old and icy. At the top of the hill the road heads north around a curve and into the west end of the campground.

BANCO BONITO ROAD:
Class I   5 miles   Elevation: 8,200-8,000 feet

On the south side of the highway, at the parking area for Redondo Campground, follow a road southeast across the opening until it climbs a hill and connects to the Banco Bonito Road, an old logging road. Not too far down the road you can climb the ridge to the west for a view of the Jemez River Valley. The road continues in an easy ski tour of about 5 miles round-trip.

Jemez Mountains—East Fork Area

EAST FORK RIDGE TRAIL—MISTLETOE CANYON TRAIL—LOS CONCHAS BURN TRAIL:
Class II $8^1/2$ miles   Elevation: 8,100-8,600 feet

There are actually three loop trails in this East Fork (of the Jemez River) ski area which all connect from a west trailhead and east trailhead off New Mexico 4. The west trailhead lies 6.4 miles east of the La Cueva junction on NM 4, and provides access to both the East Fork Ridge Trail and Mistletoe Canyon Trail. The east trailhead lies 8.9 miles from La Cueva and provides access to Las Conchas Burn Trail and the eastern most loop of East Fork Ridge Trail.

EAST FORK RIDGE TRAIL:

East Fork Ridge Trail follows the blue blazes from the parking area to the fenceline, where you can either take your skis off and pass through the gate, or turn north and follow the fenceline to the opening at the forest road that also begins in this area. Blue blazes continue to mark the route as this trail heads toward the ridge of the river canyon in a gentle ascent through ponderosa pine and over birms that keep the four-wheel drivers out in the summertime. At about the $1/2$-mile mark you reach the first junction with Mistletoe Canyon Trail, heading south towards the highway. Continue east along the ridgeline of the canyon as the trail climbs along an easy 2-mile ascent to the Las Conchas burn area. A sign marks an overlook just before you reach the burn area, where East Fork Ridge Trail meets Mistletoe Canyon Trail (near the mistletoe eradication sign). Mistletoe Canyon Trail loops around to the southwest, follows Mistletoe Canyon for several miles, zigzags south near NM 4, and then climbs back up to the East Fork Ridge Trail.

East Fork Ridge Trail continues east through stands of aspen to the junction with Las Conchas Burn Trail ascending from the east trailhead on NM 4. Continue east on East Fork Ridge Trail to a long downhill swoop through the trees which brings you to the junction of the middle and eastern loop trails in a small clearing.

The 2-mile eastern loop is more difficult than the west loop but provides some fun downhill glides and moderate uphill climbs. Bear left, to the east, as the route follows an old logging road downhill. At the bottom of the hill the trail follows a short but steep climb up the ridge to an arrow which indicates a turn south. Follow the blazes up into the trees where the trail begins to circle back to the southeast. It's an easy route along here to a short downhill section which turns north and brings you back to the small clearing described earlier where the east and middle loop trails meet.

The middle loop trail heads west here and brings you back to Las Conchas Burn Trail. Follow the blazes downhill, through the trees, in a steep descent to another old logging road. This short section of trail is rather treacherous if crusty or icy. It levels out once it reaches the road, which descends more gradually to Las Conchas Burn Trail. You can ski up the Burn Trail (described in the next section) to the East Fork Ridge Trail and follow this trail east back to the junction of the east and middle loops to complete this inner loop.

MISTLETOE CANYON TRAIL:

You can ski Mistletoe Canyon Trail in conjunction with the west end of East Fork Ridge Trail to make a loop tour starting and ending at the west trailhead.

Pick up Mistletoe Canyon Trail in the burn area and follow it south where it follows a logging road in an exhilarating downhill run of about $1/4$ mile. The run levels out in a clearing near the highway (a spur trail leads south up to the highway); follow the

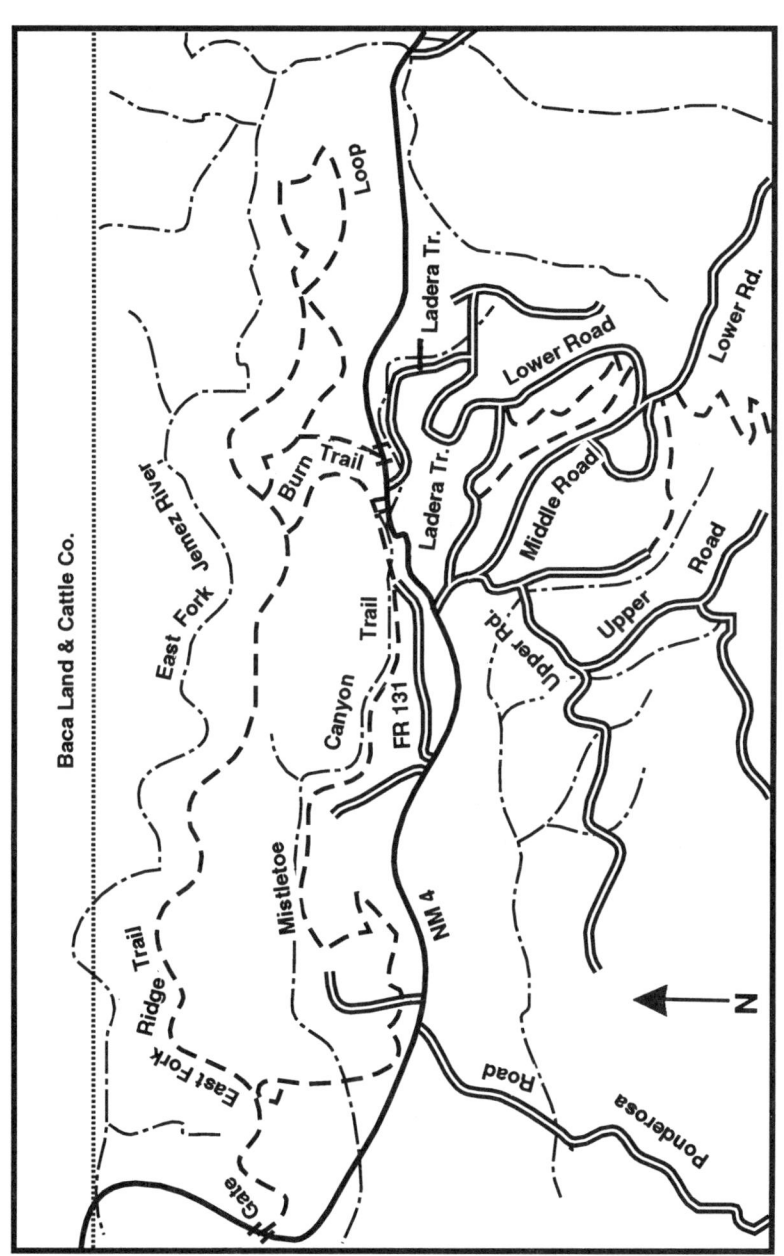

EAST FORK—LOS GRIEGOS

trail west, uphill. The trail crosses old logging roads which can cause some confusion, so be careful to follow the blazes through the trees.

The trail crosses the south side of a large meadow where FR 131 descends from the highway. Follow the trail west as it picks up another logging road. This would be a long, fun descent except for the birms in the road which periodically slow you down (placed there to prohibit summertime use of the road by four-wheel drives) and cause great consternation for those unable to negotiate short, steep hills (it once took us fifteen minutes to extract a student stuck head first in a birm during a snowstorm). The road continues for about a mile to a sharp turn south (marked with an arrow), where it climbs up from the road and circles around to the southwest. Another downhill glide brings you to a large meadow where you can see NM 4 to your left. Cross the meadow to the northwest where the trail climbs up the East Fork ridge in a series of switchbacks until it levels out and meets East Fork Ridge Trail at the top. It's about $1/2$ mile west to the trailhead on NM 4.

LAS CONCHAS BURN TRAIL:

Las Conchas Burn Trail is accessed off the east trailhead and leads to the east and middle loops of the East Fork Ridge Trail. Las Conchas Burn Trail heads northwest through a gate about one-half mile to the junction with the East Fork Ridge Trail in the burn area. You'll pass the middle loop trail junction at about a quarter mile, while Las Conchas Burn Trail continues through the aspen to the top of the ridge. Here the East Fork Ridge Trail heads both east and west (and Mistletoe Canyon Trail, about one-eighth mile west of this junction, heads south).

Jemez Mountains—Los Griegos Area

UPPER LOS GRIEGOS ROAD:
Class II-III   6.8 miles   Elevation:8,400-9,400 feet

The trailhead lies 8.4 miles from the La Cueva junction on NM 4. All three roads, upper, middle, and lower, are accessed from this gate. Upper Los Griegos Road continues south past the junctions with Lower Griego Road, at about an eighth of a mile from the highway, and just beyond that, the junction with Middle Griegos Road. Upper Los Griegos Road ascends and descends as it crosses Los Griegos Mountain and eventually junctions with Peralta-Peliza Trail at the north end of Peliza Canyon.

LOWER LOS GRIEGOS ROAD:
Class II   6 miles   Elevation: 8,400-9,100 feet

The trailhead lies 8.4 miles from La Cueva junction on NM 4. Follow Upper Los Griegos Road about an eighth of a mile and turn east (left) onto Lower Griegos Road. The road continues east across Black Dog Canyon, then junctions with Ladera Trail just north of the power lines. Turn southeast and follow Lower Road as it ascends towards Griegos Junction (it passes the continuation of Ladera Trail to the southwest). From the junction, in a large open area, Lower Road continues south for another $1^1/2$ miles.

MIDDLE LOS GRIEGOS ROAD:
Class III $2^1/2$ miles   Elevation: 8,400-9,100 feet

The most difficult of the three Los Griegos roads, Middle Road is accessed at the same gate as the Upper and Lower roads, 8.4 miles from the La Cueva junction on NM 4. Ski along the upper road, past the turn-off to Lower Griegos Road to just north of the powerlines where Middle Road turns southeast. It climbs to the junction with Lower Road at a little over a mile.

LADERA TRAIL:
Class I-II   2 miles   Elevation: 8,400-8,600 feet

This trail lies 8.9 miles from the La Cueva junction on NM 4, at the plowed parking area on the south side of the highway (just before Las Conchas Burn Trail on the north side of the highway). The first part of Ladera Trail has been blazed by the New Mexico Ski Touring Club, and the rest of the trail, to Griegos Junction, is due to be blazed as this book goes to press.

To ski the first part of the trail, pick up the blazes on an old section of NM 4, which leads a short distance east to an old logging road that follows the canyon bottom east and then south to the junction with another road; turn west (right) uphill, (Elk Ridge Trail turns east) and follow the road in a long switchback to the junction with Lower Los Griegos Road. The next section of Ladera Trail, when cleared and blazed, will lead southeast to the Griegos Junction area, in a route less steep than Upper and Lower Los Griegos roads. You can contact the Jemez Ranger Station to find out if the trail has been blazed.

Jemez Mountains—Peralta Canyon Area

CORRAL CANYON TRAIL—MEDIO DIA OVERLOOK—CALZADA TRAIL:
Class II-III   4 miles   Elevation: 8,600-9,000 feet

This is a loop through the popular Peralta Canyon area, suitable for intermediate to advanced skiers. There are other routes in the area which I will mention as this tour joins with these alternate trails.

Corral Canyon Trail was blazed by the New Mexico Ski Touring Club and the Forest Service after Peralta Canyon Road (Forest Road 280) began to be plowed for access to new television towers. The loop described here goes up Corral Canyon, crosses Peralta Canyon Road, continues to the junction of Forest Road 282, and on to Medio Dia Overlook above the Valle Grande. The return route follows FR 282 or Corral Canyon Trail to Peralta Canyon Road,

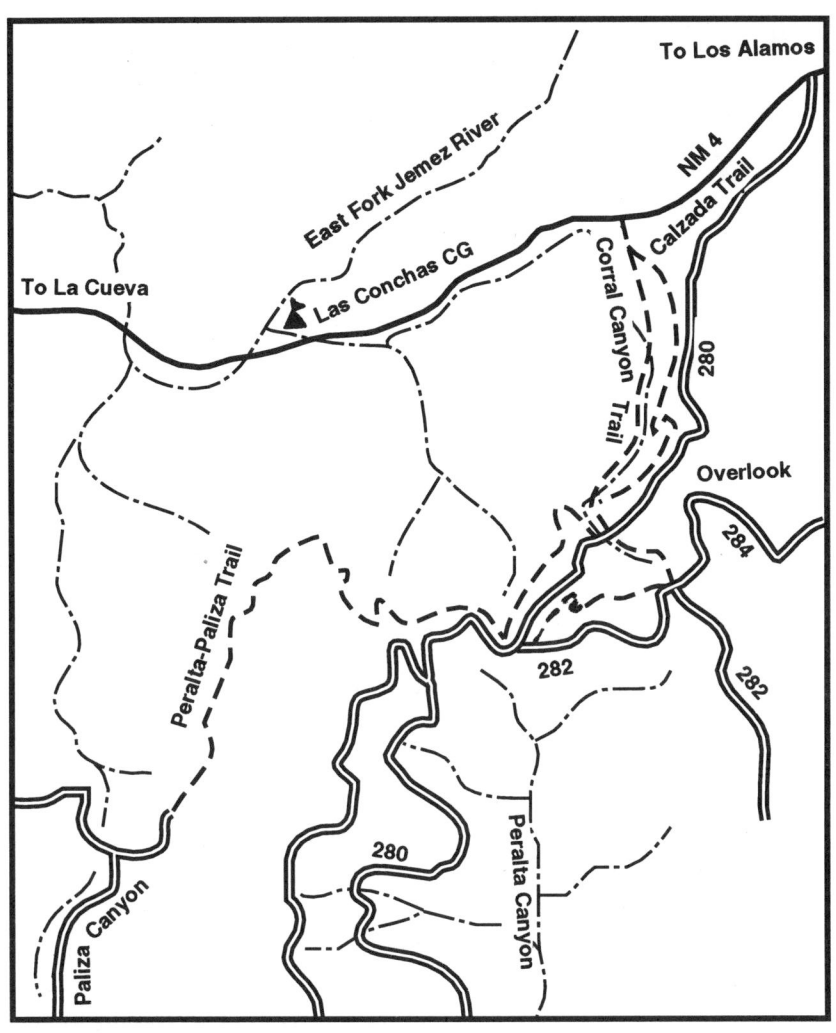

PERALTA CANYON AREA

and along Calzada Trail back down to New Mexico 4.

The Corral Canyon trailhead is 11.7 miles east on NM 4 from the La Cueva junction of NM 4 and NM 126. There is room to park your car at the gate leading to the trail (marked more difficult and blazed with blue cross-country diamonds) and at another gate

Corral in meadow on Corral Canyon Trail

about 50 yards farther along the highway (from this gate an old road leads up to Peralta Canyon Road). A sign indicates the turn left to Calzada Trail, while Corral Canyon Trail heads south 1 mile, directly up the canyon. The trail travels through a meadow where you can practice snowplow and telemark turns on the wide, gentle hills. About a quarter mile up you pass the trail's namesake, the corrals barely visible in the deep Jemez snow. Depressions in the snow indicate the creek that flows through the meadow.

The trail steepens as it enters the trees, paralleling Peralta Canyon Road to the east, along the ridge of the canyon. There's a detour to the left around the steepest part of the canyon; a sign indicates the turn left. Just before you reach Junction Meadow, Calzada Trail joins with Corral Canyon Trail. In the meadow, Corral Canyon Trail turns east, towards Peralta Canyon Road, and Calzada Trail continues south, into the trees. At the road and to the left is its origin at NM 4; to the right the road continues on to

Peralta Canyon. Corral Canyon Trail continues directly across the road (follow the blue blazes) and up into the trees.

At the next meadow, another good practice area, you're only a few short hills from the junction of FR 282. There's a sign here declaring this road "unmaintained." To the left, your destination, FR 282 is a fairly level route leading about a half mile to the Medio Dia Canyon Overlook. To the right, FR 282 leads downhill to Peralta Canyon Road.

Follow FR 282 north (left) around the ridge to the Overlook at the north-south fenceline. The view extends to the Sangre de Cristos above the vast Jemez Caldera. It's a good place to pound down some snow for a seat and eat lunch. Forest Road 282 continues east from here, downhill into Medio Dia Canyon, and eventually leads back to NM 4, 11 miles later. There is a shortcut along this route, $1^1/2$ miles from the overlook, which leads north up an old logging road, then down the ridge along a fenceline to NM 4.

After lunch your route returns south along either FR 282 or the continuation of Corral Canyon Trail across the ridge to FR 280. At the "unmaintained" sign, follow 282 southwest down the side of the canyon. It's a nice glide down 282 to Peralta Canyon Road, if conditions haven't deteriorated too much on this exposed road. On a clear day you can see all the way south to the Sandia Mountains. Be careful coming down to the junction of Peralta Road. One of my students once broke a ski tip zooming down into the icy snowbank alongside the road. To follow Corral Canyon Trail instead of FR 282, follow the blue blazes leading west into the trees at the "unmaintained" sign. The trail passes through a meadow where views extend south to the Sandia Mountains, then switchbacks around the north side of the ridge and continues southwest to the junction with FR 282 and FR 280.

You can use Calzada Trail as your route back down the canyon. Blue blazes on the west side of the road indicate the trail; Calzada Trail heads north, down through the trees, while Peralta-Peliza Trail heads west in a 2-mile tour. The blazes are evident as you come to the junction of the roads. Follow them into the trees across Peralta Canyon Road. The first downhill glide brings you to a fairly level trail through the trees. The route continues north, alongside the road, until a switchback (marked on a tree with arrows) brings you down the side of Corral Canyon to the junction with Corral Canyon Trail in Junction Meadow.

Follow the trail down Corral Canyon to where Calzada trail turns east, (right), into the trees (marked more difficult, while Corral Canyon Trail is marked most difficult). This trail traverses the side of the canyon, basically paralleling Corral Canyon Trail. An upper switchback momentarily takes you higher into the trees. The rest of the trail is a nice glide back to the junction with Corral Canyon Trail at the trailhead. More advanced skiers can return on Corral Canyon Trail for a faster run down the canyon, but be careful on the steep parts of the trail—use your snowplow to avoid intimate contact with the trees.

PERALTA-PELIZA TRAIL:
Class II   4 miles   Elevation: 9,200-9,500 feet

This route, which connects with the Corral Canyon and Calzada trails, can be skied into the Peliza Canyon area in conjunction with the Corral Canyon-Medio Dia route. The trailhead lies at the junction of Forest Roads 280 and 282 where Calzada Trail terminates.

Follow the blue blazes west as the trail climbs into the trees. An uphill climb follows close to the electronic site road; just past where you actually see the road a view north extends to the Valle Grande. Watch for several switchbacks as you continue climbing west to a meadow; cross the meadow and pick up the trail again at the north side where it reenters the trees.

The trail continues climbing to the top of the Las Conchas Ridge where it turns south, and momentarily levels out. From here views open up to Redondo Peak and the Jemez East Fork River valley. The trail follows the ridge south through thick spruce-fir vegetation (the trail is narrow and sloped), climbing to the junction with a logging road at the north end of Paliza

Canyon.

LAS CONCHAS TRAIL:
Class II   2.6 miles   Elevation: 8,500-9,200 feet

This is an alternate route to Peralta Canyon, named by Sam Beard of the New Mexico Ski Touring Club. It begins on the south side of New Mexico 4, across the road from Las Conchas Campground (10.8 miles from the La Cueva junction). The route follows an old hiking trail southeast to the intersection of Peralta Canyon Road and Forest Road 282 in a little more than a mile.

Jemez Mountains—St. Peter's Dome Area

DEL NORTE CANYON:
Class II   6-22 miles   Elevation: 8,600-9,000 feet

Forest Road 268 to Del Norte Canyon intersects New Mexico 4 about 14 miles east of the La Cueva junction of NM 126 and NM 4. You can ski this road south to the junction of Forest Road 283 (3 miles) and on to Medio dia Canyon, the destination of the Corral Canyon-Peralta Canyon route described earlier (11 miles).

ST. PETER'S DOME, FOREST ROAD 289:
Class I   5 miles   Elevation: 8,900-8,800 feet

This Forest Road is an easy tour that eventually leads to Dome Lookout. The road intersects New Mexico 4 about 18 miles east of the La Cueva junction. It's 2 1/2 miles along FR 289 to the junction with Forest Road 287, which leads to Frijoles Ridge above Bandelier National Monument.

UPPER FRIJOLES SKI TRAILS:
Class I   21/2-5 miles   Elevation: 8,900-8,700 feet

This system of loop trails lies just east of St. Peter's Dome Road in Bandelier National Monument, just over 18 miles from the La Cueva junction on NM 4 (36.8 miles from Pojoaque via NM 502 and NM 4 if you're coming from northern New Mexico). Two easy loop trails travel around the west end of Upper Frijoles Canyon, affording views down into the canyon. No permit is necessary, but there is a sign-in box at the trailhead, where you can also find maps of the routes. There is a parking area on the north side of the highway, across from the trailhead.

The shorter of the two trails heads east from the trailhead, where a sign tells you it's 1.2 miles to the scenic overlook. Follow the blue trail markers along the wide, gentle route to the first junction of Loop E, where an arrow guides you to the right, along the south side of the loop. This leads to the overlook on the north side of Upper Frijoles Canyon. The loop turns to the west and continues back to the E marker on the tree, where an arrow guides you left, along the southern portion of Loop F. The loop terminates just to the south of where you started at NM 4.

The longer route, 5 miles, heads southwest from the trailhead in another easy tour to two different overlooks. Red blazes mark the route as it travels toward St. Peter's Dome Road. At the fenceline it turns south and skirts the west end of Upper Frijoles Canyon. There's a spur trail marked A leading left to the first overlook on the south side of the canyon. From here the trail quickly leads to the first junction, Loop B, where an arrow points you left along the east side of the loop. You'll soon reach Loop C, where again an arrow points you left along the south side. The second overlook spur trail is marked by D.

Loop C continues around to the west as it returns toward Loop B. The return to the highway is longer than the route out and is mostly uphill, although quite gentle. At Loop B an arrow guides you left along the south side of the loop as it circles back to the first part of the trail, where you retrace your route back toward the fenceline and highway.

Jemez Mountains—San Pedro Parks Area

BLUEBIRD MESA
Class I-II   Variable mileage   Elevation: 8,700-9,200 feet

Located on the north side of the Jemez range outside the town of Cuba, Bluebird Mesa offers gentle touring and spectacular views on top of a mesa criss-crossed by forest roads. To find FR 98, which accesses Bluebird Mesa, take NM 126 east from the town of Cuba 11.4 miles to the end of the pavement. A parking pull-off on the south side of the highway marks the trailhead.

Forest Road 98 climbs southeast to the top of the mesa in a gentle 1-mile ascent. Where the road levels out, two routes are available: the logging road to the east (left) leads across the mesa top for several miles; the road to the right (southwest) can be skied to a great view of the Sandia Mountains or on as a loop back to NM 126 (this area is logged and the returning road is oftentimes ruined by truck marks).

VACAS TRAIL:
Class II-III   9 miles   Elevation: 8,400-9,500 feet

The San Pedro Parks Wilderness is in one of the more remote areas of the Jemez Mountains, and provides excellent cross-country skiing. Access can be a problem, though, along Forest Road 264, a steep, winding road leading 2.7 miles to the wilderness boundary.

To reach the Vacas Trailhead, one of the main entrances into the wilderness, take New Mexico 126 east from the town of Cuba 12 miles to FR 264. This dirt road heads north to San Pedro Parks, and is unmaintained during the winter months. It can be quite icy, due to a southern exposure, and is an uphill climb to the wilderness boundary.

At Vacas Trail there is a large parking area, and Forest Service signs describe San Pedro Parks and the origin of San Gregorio Reservoir. The trip to the reservoir is easy, approximately 1 mile north along a wide, canopied path. At the reservoir, in a large

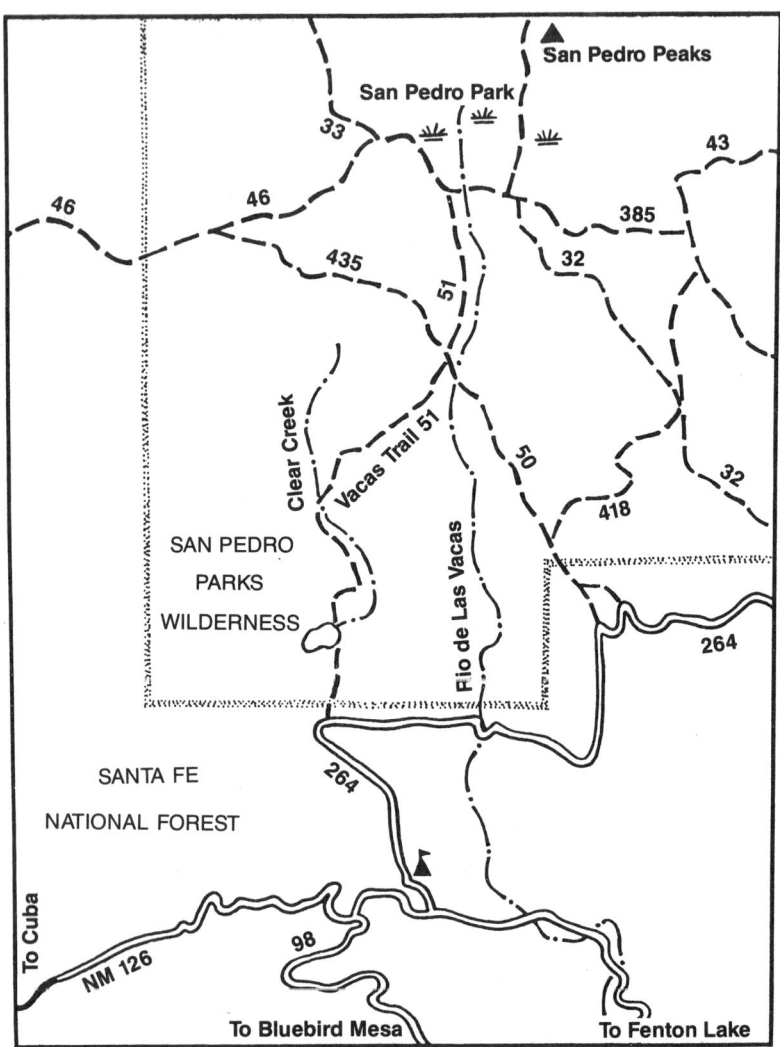

SAN PEDRO PARKS

meadow, the trail becomes less obvious. There are two possible routes to the main trail leading northeast to Clear Creek. The trail to the right, through the trees, is apt to provide better snow conditions in the shade of the spruce-fir vegetation. This route follows the east edge of the meadow to a sign stating that camping and open fires are prohibited at the reservoir. The other route travels north across the reservoir meadow until it turns into the trees at the far north end and connects, at the same sign, with the trail coming through the trees.

From the sign Vacas Trail heads northeast up an easy incline to Clear Creek. Cross the creek (easily negotiated) to the east side and follow the creek north in a relatively gentle ascent. About a mile later Clear Creek forks and Vacas Trail follows the right fork through a high alpine meadow ringed by spruce, fir, and aspen. At the north end of the meadow the trail crosses the creek again and heads north into the trees.

From here to the Anastacio-Palomas trails' junction, Vacas Trail winds its way north across several ridges and through beautiful meadows to the Rio de las Vacas in another large meadow. The trail crosses the river to the east side, where a sign marks the junction of Palomas Trail #50 heading southeast. (Palomas trailhead is about 4 miles farther east from the Vacas trailhead on FR 264.)

Vacas Trail continues north along the river valley for about a quarter mile where it recrosses the river and meets Anastacio Trail #435 heading west. Anastacio Trail, 3.3 miles in length, is a connecting trail between Vacas Trail and Los Pinos Trail #46, which originates on Forest Road 95, also out of Cuba.

Vacas Trail continues north along the river another $2^1/_2$ miles to San Pedro Parks, the heart of the wilderness. Other trails lead north, west, and east out of the park. The entire route from the Vacas trailhead to the park is 9 miles; add another 2.7 miles along FR 264 and you have a much longer route than you can comfortably ski in a day. Depending upon the condition of FR 264 and your skiing ability, you can choose to ski as far as you like on this route, then enjoy the downhill trip back to your car. I recommend skiing as far as Clear Creek, then turning back. This tour is approximately 9 miles round-trip. For those of you who are experienced enough to undertake a two-day outing, you can reach the Rio de las Vacas and follow it into the park as far as you like.

SANTA FE NATIONAL FOREST

Sangre de Cristo Mountains

The eastern portion of Santa Fe National Forest encompasses the vast Pecos Wilderness, and many of the ski trails described below are in or near the wilderness. While most of these trails are more appropriate for the intermediate or advanced skier, there are also beginner trails in both the Santa Fe Ski Basin and Cowles areas. All the trails provide good snow conditions, beautiful scenery, and relatively easy access.

The Santa Fe Ski Basin lies 18 miles northeast of Santa Fe on Hyde Park Road (FR 101). All of that area's trails described below are accessed off this road. The Cowles area, on the Pecos side of the mountains, is reached via I-25 to the Pecos-Glorieta exit. Follow NM 50 6 miles to the town of Pecos; turn left onto NM 63 and it's 20 miles to Cowles. NM 63 is paved only as far as Terrero, but is usually snowplowed to Cowles.

Sangre de Cristo Mountains—Santa Fe Ski Basin

BLACK CANYON CAMPGROUND:
Class I 1 mile Elevation: 8,300-8,400 feet

This is a perfect beginner area, located only a short distance from Santa Fe on the ski basin road. Take Hyde Park Road off Washington Street in Santa Fe 7^1/$_2$ miles to the entrance to the campground on the east side of the highway.

The campground road provides a gentle ascent through the campground, about ^{1}/$_2$ mile in length, to a loop at the end of the area. It's appropriate for beginning skiers to practice both uphill technique as well as downhill skills back to the highway. A trail leads up into the forest at the east end of the campground, but quickly becomes too steep for the novice skier.

PACHECO CANYON ROAD, FR 102:
Class II   6-10 miles   Elevation: 9,700-7,700 feet

Forest Road 102 leads into Pacheco Canyon where it connects with FR 412, which in turn leads to Aspen Meadows, access to the Pecos Wilderness. You can ski a 3-mile tour to the junction of the forest roads, or ski another 2 miles to Aspen Meadow.

Take Hyde Park Road off Washington Street in Santa Fe 12 miles to FR 102 on the west side of the highway. The road descends into Pacheco Canyon through spruce-fir forest for 3 miles to the junction with FR 412, which turns north and travels another 2 miles before crossing the creek and entering the meadow area.

ASPEN VISTA, FOREST ROAD 150:
Class I-II   6-12 miles   Elevation: 10,000-12,000 feet

This forest road route can be either a great downhill adventure or a leisurely-paced round-trip of whatever mileage you choose. It begins on Hyde Park Road to the Santa Fe Ski Basin and ascends to the top of the ski area.

Take Hyde Park Road off Washington Street in Santa Fe $15^{1}/2$ miles northeast to the Aspen Vista Recreation Site where Forest Road 150 begins. The tour up the road is a steady 6-mile climb to the top of the Big Tesuque Ski Run. If you want some downhill thrills without the uphill work, you can drive to the ski basin ($1^{1}/2$ miles beyond Aspen Vista) and take the red chairlift to the triple chair at midway, which in turn takes you to the top of the mountain. This is an expensive one-way ride, however, as the ski basin requires that you buy a one-way ticket for each chair, the red and the triple, to reach the top of the mountain. Obviously, they are discouraging cross-country skiers from using ski basin facilities. They also prohibit cross-country skiers from ascending the eastern most forest road slope as access to the triple chair. If you do decide to ride the lifts, as you come off the chair stay along the rim of the mountains west to the Big Tesuque Trail. Both the upper and lower sections of this trail lead to the junction of Aspen Vista

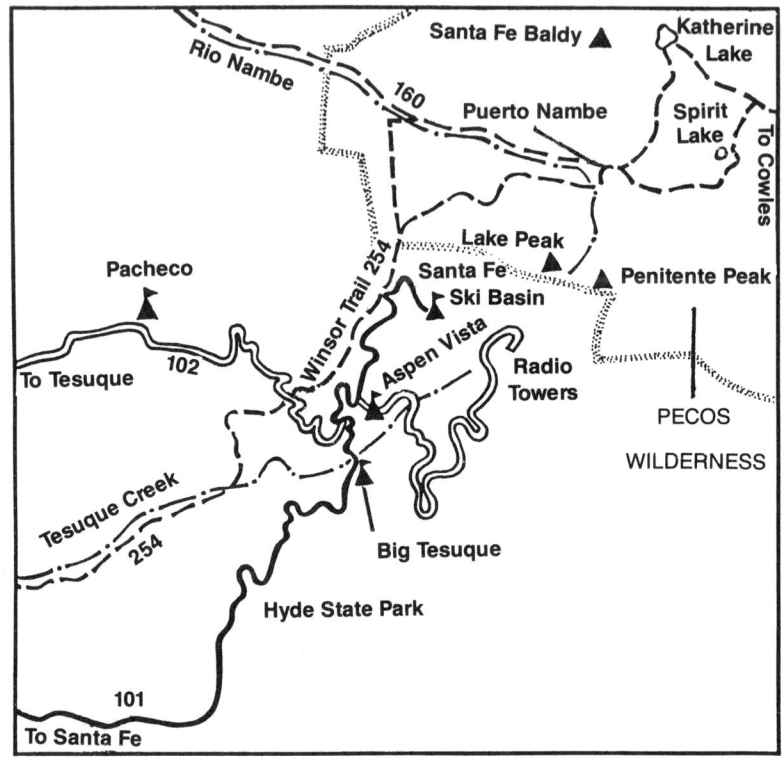

SANTA FE SKI BASIN: ASPEN VISTA; PACHECO CANYON; WINSOR TRAIL

Road.

If you decide to ski up the road and back, the views will reward your effort. It's a moderate climb along the road to the southeast, through the famous aspens now devoid of leaf. Soon you'll see a panorama of the Jemez Mountains and Rio Grande Valley to the west. The road climbs out of the aspen and into the spruce-fir vegetation as it turns around the ridge to the northeast, at about the 3½-mile mark. Views of both the Rio Grande Valley and the Santa Fe area open up as the road switchbacks in and out of the trees. As you near the top you can see the chairlift to the northwest and the microwave towers on Tesuque Peak to the northeast. Lake Peak looms straight ahead.

The run back down is wide enough to practice telemark turns, but not so steep that you can't point your skis down the hill and go for it. Uphill skiers need to beware of those speed demons coming down.

NORSKI TRACKS DE SANTA FE:
Class I-II   5 kilometers   Elevation: 10,000 feet

This loop trail near the ski basin was laid out in 1985 by a Santa Fe ski touring club in conjunction with several sporting goods stores. It is very well marked with blue cross-country diamond blazes, a trailhead map, and distance markers, and includes both a beginner's loop and a longer, connecting intermediate loop. The trailhead lies 16 miles northeast of Santa Fe on Hyde Park Road (about a half mile before the Santa Fe Ski Basin parking lot), on the west side of the highway. There is a pull-off for cars, a sign posting cross-country ski ethics, and a map of the trailhead a little farther up the trail. Arrows on the sign guide skiers northeast (right) on the loop, into the dense stands of aspen that cover the mountain.

Most of the first part of this trail is moderate downhill terrain. A series of "crossover" signs mark the junctions of the returning trail as it passes by the forward route: stop signs on this return trail prevent wrong-way access; arrows to the right keep the skier in the forward direction. At the fifth crossover, a sign directs beginners, back to the trailhead on the return route. A "more difficult" sign directs intermediate skiers to the right along the slightly more difficult terrain. Caution signs mark several steep hills, and a bypass provides more level terrain at one of the hills.

The next trail sign indicates an overlook. This bypass leads to the right along a narrow, steep trail down to a rather obscured overlook of the Jemez Mountains to the west. This side trip may not be worth it for those skiers leery of negotiating a narrow run through the trees, although some exposed rocks at the overlook provide a good lunch spot. The main trail continues to the left (you're now heading east, back toward the trailhead). The return trip is mostly uphill, occasionally requiring a herringbone technique. Flagging on trees .mark the 2,500- and 3,000-meter distances, and the last 500 meters can be full of bare spots due to its southern exposure. The trail converges with the beginning loop at the trailhead marker. There is no risk of the unexpected or losing the trail on this carefully laid out route. The trail is groomed wide enough to allow for skating technique.

WINSOR TRAIL:
Class III   10 miles   Elevation: 10,000-11,000 feet

Winsor Trail offers some of the best back-country skiing and most spectacular vistas in all of New Mexico. You can travel as far as you like on this trail that goes all the way to Cowles on the east side of the Pecos Wilderness, but a good day's round-trip can be made to Puerto Nambe, the saddle below Santa Fe Baldy. There is some discrepancy on the Forest Service signs as to the distance, but I'd say the trail to Puerto Nambe is between 4 and 5 miles, so a round-trip tour is almost 10 miles.

The Winsor trailhead is located at the north end of the lower Santa Fe Ski Basin parking lot, designated by Forest Service signs. The trail crosses a creek and turns northeast up a precipitous, switchbacking half mile to the Pecos Wilderness boundary. Don't let this half mile discourage you—it's absolutely the most difficult part of the trail. If conditions are bad you might want to remove your skis and hike to where the trail levels out near the uppermost switchbacks. You can also bypass the lower switchbacks by skiing up an open area just east of the upper parking lot to the barrier posts on the trail.

At the top of the ridge the trail enters the wilderness. Immediately you descend in a gentle glide east through the trees, on the northwest side of the ridge. You'll begin to catch glimpses of the Jemez Mountains to the west as you enjoy this exhilarating downhill run. About one-half mile along the trail is the junction of Forest Trail 403, which leads 1³/₄ miles to Rio Nambe Trail, a trail that follows the Rio Nambe and intersects Winsor Trail at Puerto Nambe.

Views start to display the full range of the Jemez Mountains from Redondo Peak to Tres Piedras. As the evergreens give way to aspen groves, the trail turns east affording the first glimpses of the high Pecos peaks. The route is still mostly downhill to the backside of the Santa Fe Ski Basin. In a large bowl the trail turns north again through the aspen, leveling out. You pass the junction of the La Vega shortcut, also leading to Rio Nambe Trail.

The route turns east again toward the Puerto Nambe saddle. From a meadow on the ridge below the saddle you can see the magnificent Santa Fe Baldy, standing cold and barren to the north. The trail enters the trees again on the east side of the meadow; a Forest Service sign says it's 4 miles back to the Ski Basin and three-quarters of a mile to Puerto Nambe. Down in the trees the trail crosses a stream of the Rio Nambe and immediately begins the ascent of the open slopes of the ridge to Puerto Nambe.

Be careful to follow the trail as it turns northwest across the snowfields up to the north side of the ridge (previous ski tracks can quickly be covered up by blowing snow on this open terrain). You feel like this could be one of those remote Alaskan bowls you see in the travelogues: skiers lifted to the top of the mountain come telemarking down in clouds of snow. On the north side of the ridge the trail turns east again toward the saddle. Stop here and take a rest after the snowfield climb, as Santa Fe Baldy looms right there above you to the north, and Penitente Peak and Lake Peak rise to the south. One last climb brings you to the Puerto Nambe saddle, where the east and west Pecos meet at the junction of Rio Nambe Trail and Forest Trail 251 to Lake Katherine. Winsor Trail continues to Spirit Lake and Stewart Lake, far below you to the east. You're at the crossroads here, in the middle of the high Pecos country that makes this Winsor Trail trip so wonderful.

The return trip can seem intimidating, remembering those wonderful downhill glides that you will now have to go up, but none of the hills are that steep, and there is enough diversity of terrain to provide some return downhill thrill, too. You may again want to avoid the final, treacherous half mile and turn off the trail at the barrier posts to ski down the open slope under the powerline.

Sangre de Cristo Mountains—Cowles Area

IRON GATE CAMPGROUND:
Class II-III   8-11 miles   Elevation: 8,000-10,000 feet

There are several cross-country skiing areas on the east side of the Pecos Wilderness, accessible from the village of Pecos. Forest Road 223 can be skied to Iron Gate Campground (4 miles) and those skiers with the stamina to continue can take Forest Trail 249 to Hamilton Mesa (another $1^1/2$ miles).

Take I-25 to the Pecos-Glorieta exit. It's 6 miles to the village of Pecos where you turn left on New Mexico 63. Follow this road 19 miles (1 mile before the village of Cowles) to the Iron Gate Campground Road.

Forest Road 223 to Iron Gate Campground is mostly an uphill, northeasterly climb through a summer home area and section of private land. The first part of the road is fairly steep, up to the summer homes. Stay to the right at the half-mile mark where a spur road forks to the left. The road levels out somewhat as you pass the summer cabins, and views open up over your shoulder of the high Pecos peaks to the west—Santa Fe Baldy, Pecos Baldy, and the Truchas peaks. When you reach the Iron Gate Campground direction sign, the road leads uphill again, but then levels out to the Circle S stables. From here it's only another mile to the campground.

If you're ready for further adventure by the time you reach the campground, you can take FT 249 to Hamilton Mesa, a beautiful meadow area with views to the west. Ski to the northeast end of the campground to find the trail. A Forest Service sign here says it's $1^1/2$ miles to Hamilton Mesa, $5^1/2$ miles to Beatty's Cabin (named for the intrepid 19th-century prospector whose cabin used to sit near where the Forest Service and Game and Fish cabins do now), and 8 miles to Pecos Falls. The tour to Hamilton Mesa is within the limits of the experienced, energetic skier, and is worth the effort.

The trail climbs moderately to the northeast, a quarter mile to the junction of the spur trail to the right to Grass Mountain. Stay to the left and the trail becomes quite level as it follows the rim of the canyon overlooking the Mora River down to the right. There's a nice glide down into an aspen grove away from the rim, then the trail returns to the edge of the canyon and passes through a stand of huge ponderosa pine. About three-quarters of a mile beyond is the junction of Forest Trail 250 to Mora Flats (2 miles). This trail follows the river to the right, and the trail to Hamilton Mesa continues to the left.

The last part of the trail is steeper than the previous part of the trail, and you might want to stop here and turn around for the return trip. Forest Trail 249 continues up to a Forest Service fence, then enters Hamilton Mesa, a huge alpine meadow stretching to the northeast. As you climb to the aspen grove above you the whole range of the Pecos peaks once again appears to the west. The snow in the meadow can be quite crusty and icy due to exposure, so unless there's some fresh snow and you want to practice some telemarking, it's time to turn around and begin the $5^1/2$-mile trip back. Forest Trail 249 also branches west at the campground and follows the Pecos River down to Cowles, but this is a steep return route and is not recommended.

CAVE CREEK TRAIL:
Class II   6 miles   Elevation: 8,100-8,800 feet

This is a wonderful cross-country excursion into the Pecos Wilderness to the hidden caves filled with the rushing waters of Cave Creek. The trail continuously parallels Cave Creek or Panchuela Creek and is subsequently easy to follow. The terrain is moderate.

Take New Mexico 63 to Cowles, make an immediate left over

the Pecos Bridge and an immediate right onto the Panchuela Campground road (designated by a Forest Service sign). This 1-mile road is unmaintained, so park the car and begin your ski tour

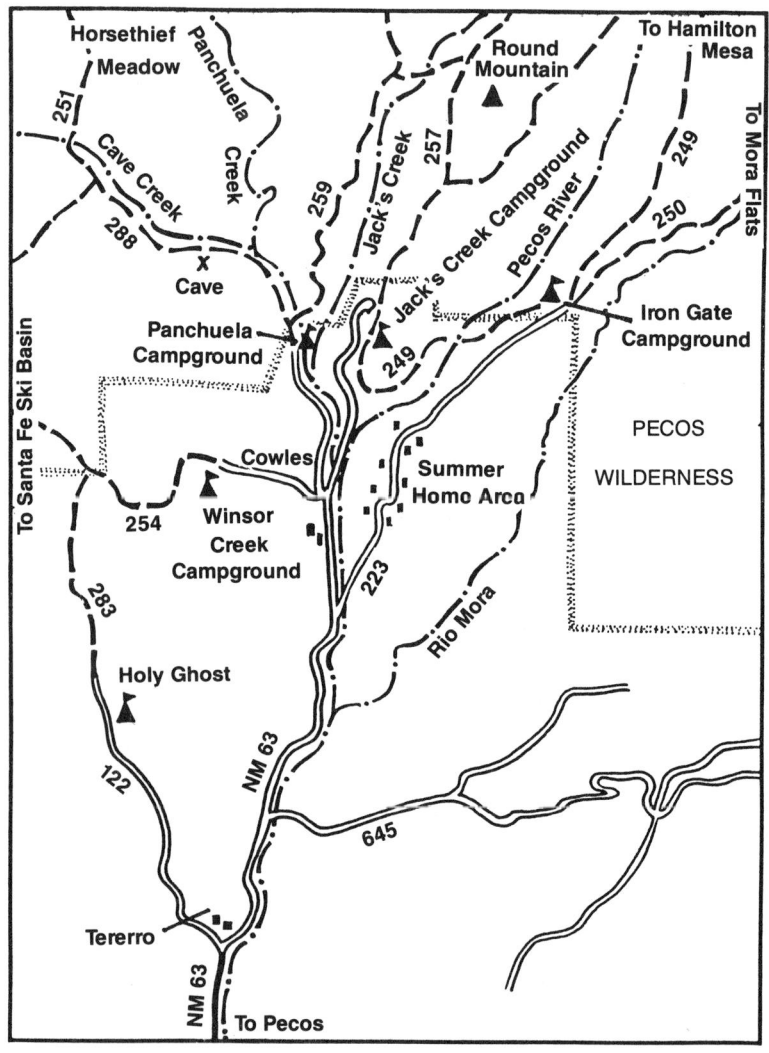

COWLES AREA: IRONGATE CAMPGROUND; CAVE CREEK; WINSOR CREEK; JACK'S CREEK

uphill through the Los Pinos Guest Ranch land to the campground sign. Cave Creek Trail #288 actually begins here, before the road descends to the campground, but to avoid having to cross Panchuela Creek on skis (a wet, cold idea), continue down into the campground and you'll find a bridge that leads over to the north side of the creek to a connecting trail.

You may want to walk this first part of the trail as it climbs to a ridge above the creek. The trail then levels out, and you'll ski through (or over, depending on the depth of the snow) a Forest Service fence before descending to the junction with Cave Creek Trail after it crosses Panchuela Creek about a quarter mile northwest of the campground. A Forest Service sign here says it's $5^1/2$ miles along FT 288 to Horsethief Meadow, 8 miles to Pecos Baldy Lake, and 9 miles to Beatty's.

Cave Creek Trails levels out through an aspen grove as it follows Panchuela Creek on the north side. Soon another trail sign indicates the junction to Pecos Baldy Lake to the right. Continue to the left, following the arrow to Horsethief Meadow. The trail remains level until a steep ascent brings you back next to the creek.

At the confluence of Panchuela and Cave creeks, the trail crosses Panchuela Creek to the left and follows Cave Creek to the west. Look for an open area marking the junction, and you'll find the logs laid across the creek for a homemade bridge. There is also a rather obscure sign here indicating Cave Creek. The trail ascends and descends quickly, then levels out into a mile's gentle climb to the caves. You can miss these completely if you don't pay attention. Look for an opening in the vegetation to the left (creekside) where the trail returns alongside the creek after a short divergence; an old hollow tree lies pointing toward the creek at the opening. Cross over to the creek and you'll find the small limestone caves—dark, clammy recesses claiming the gushing creek waters. This is a good place to eat lunch and watch the water flow before skiing the 3 miles back to Cowles.

WINSOR CREEK CAMPGROUND ROAD:
Class I   3 miles   Elevation: 8,100-8,400 feet

This forest road across the bridge at Cowles leads a mile and a half in an easy ascent to the campground, where the Winsor Trail leads up into the Pecos Wilderness to Spirit Lake. More advanced skiers may want to continue up Winsor Trail to Spirit Lake. At the parking area, follow the trail alongside Winsor Creek to the first river crossing. On the far side of the creek Winsor Trail #254 climbs the ridge out of the canyon; Trail #261 continues straight up the canyon in a steeper ascent. Winsor Trail can be skied as far as Spirit Lake, and for an overnight ski trip to Puerto Nambe.

JACK'S CREEK CAMPGROUND ROAD:
Class I-II   5 miles   Elevation: 8,100-9,300 feet

At Cowles the forest road into Jack's Creek continues north up a hill $2^1/_2$ miles to the campground. Here there are several loop roads through the campground suitable for ski touring, and several trails lead into the Pecos Wilderness: Trail #25 to Trail #257 leads to Round Mountain and on to Pecos Baldy Lake; Trail #25 leads to Beatty's Cabin.

Sangre de Cristo Mountains—Las Vegas Area

Several trails appropriate for cross-country skiing have been recently cleared and marked by a group of Las Vegas volunteers and the Forest Service. One trail is accessed out of Las Vegas, while the other trail is accessed from the small village of Ledoux, south of Mora.

CARRETON CANYON LOOP:
Class I-II   7 miles   Elevation: 7,900 feet

This loop trail lies in the Johnson Mesa area west of the town of Las Vegas. Take NM 65 northwest from Las Vegas 13 miles to the junction with NM 65, which turns right to El Porvenir Campground. Stay on NM 263 another 2.2 miles to the forest boundary, and turn left onto Johnson Mesa Road #156. Park in the campground; the road should be plowed this far. Ski up FR 156, the Johnson Mesa Road, a little more than a quarter mile until you see the "Closed for resource protection" sign. Cross over the birm and ski up this old road which parallels FR 156. It reconnects with FR 156 near the junction with Mineral Hill Road #18, at 1.7 miles. Continue up FR 156, which climbs steadily past a great view of Hermit's Peak to the north. At .9 miles an old logging road to the left indicates the turn onto the loop trail. The route follows Carreton Canyon for $2^1/_2$ miles before joining County Road #18 about a mile below the junction of #18 and FR 156. Follow #18 back to FR 156, turn right and continue back to the campground the same way you came.

FOREST ROAD 636:
Class II-III   6-13 miles

Take NM 94 south from Mora 4 miles to the village of Ledoux. At the church, turn right onto FR 635 which leads to Morphy Lake State Park. It's 1.6 miles to the turn to FR 636, where a cross-country ski sign indicates the route. Snow conditions are usually good, and FR 635 should be plowed this far.

From this junction, skiers can follow a 6-mile loop up FR 636; stay on FR 636 for 2 miles where a ski sign directs you onto an old logging road through the woods. This road works its way back down to the 2-mile mark on FR 636 (keep following the ski signs), where you can ski back down to your car. A longer, 13-mile loop can be skied by following the logging road all the way to Capulin Canyon.

CARSON NATIONAL FOREST

Sangre de Cristo Mountains—Taos Ski Valley

New Mexico's highest mountain, Wheeler Peak, rises 13,161 feet in the heart of the Wheeler Peak Wilderness area above the Taos Ski Valley. The trails leading to Wheeler take the advanced skier through some of the most spectacular scenery in New Mexico, but also some of the most difficult and avalanche prone. Skiers should always be aware of snow conditions, and check with the Taos Ski Valley or Forest Service to assess avalanche danger before attempting these climbs. Intermediate skiers can limit their trips to the first part of these trails and avoid the higher, steeper terrain.

To reach the Taos Ski Valley, drive north of Taos on NM 522 to the junction with NM 150; turn east (right) and it's 15 miles to the ski area. All the trailheads lie at the southeast corner of the parking lot.

Kachina Peak from Williams Lake Trail

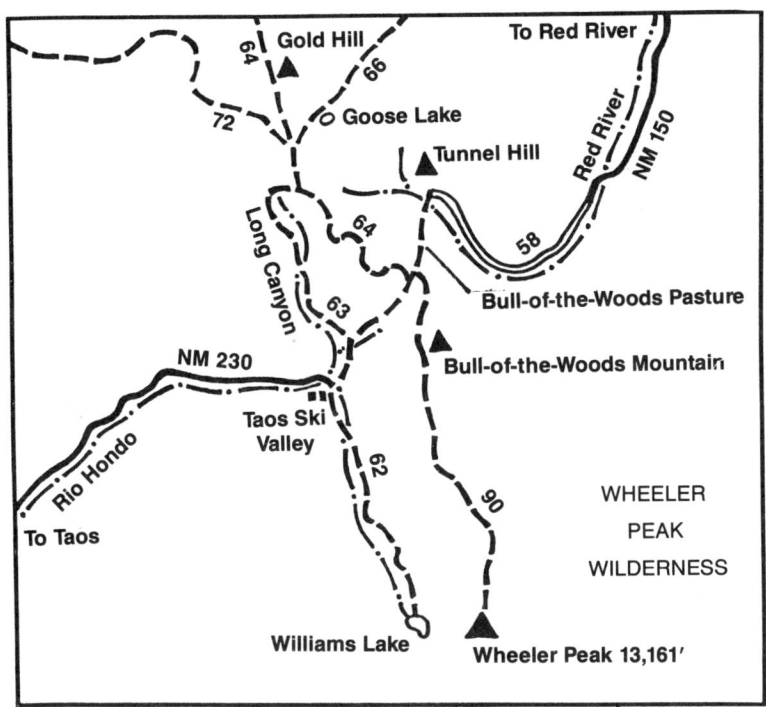

WHEELER PEAK AREA: WILLIAMS LAKE; BULL-OF-THE-WOODS; LONG CANYON

WILLIAMS LAKE TRAIL:
CLass III   9 miles   Elevation: 9,400-11,000 feet

This is the route, via Williams Lake, that most hikers take on their way to Wheeler Peak, the tallest mountain in New Mexico, 13,161 feet high. Cross-country skiers can ski to the lake, which sits in a glacial bowl 4^1/$_2$ miles from Taos Ski Valley.

From the southeast end of the ski valley parking lot ski south through the condominium and cabin area. This road is a steady climb that can be rather confusing as you pass private drives to cabins; bear south to the second switchback, a half mile from the parking lot. Here the road turns sharply north in a steep ascent. If you followed the road south instead of the switchback north you would eventually connect with a beginner ski slope descending from the restaurant and the Kachina Chairlift, your ultimate destination, but the ski area has prohibited uphill traffic between 9 a.m. and 4 p.m., so this route may be used only early in the day. The upper road you will follow is more scenic and out of the way of downhill skiers. Follow the switchback north to the next switchback south (the road continuing north leads through private land to Bull-of-the-Woods Trail) and you'll see a sign stating that this is also private land and unauthorized vehicles are not permitted beyond this point. If snow conditions permit, you can sometimes drive to this point and park, considerably shortening your climb to Williams Lake.

From here the road continues to climb for a mile and a half to the restaurant and Kachina Chairlift. You can see the lower road down in the canyon next to Lake Fork Rio Hondo. The high wilderness peaks loom ahead. At the restaurant, continue south along the stream a short distance to where the road forks; bear southeast along the stream, as the road to the right turns and circles back to the chairlift. About a half mile up, the road narrows to a trail, and a marker indicates that Williams Lake is 2 miles farther.

The trail now leaves the stream, continuing its southeast climb through the trees to a meadow. This is the beginning of the avalanche area, as the slopes steepen to the east. Behind you appear the high peaks of the Gold Hill area, and Kachina Peak is the mountain to the west. The trail passes through boulder fields and east-side talus slopes to the Wheeler Peak Wilderness boundary sign, about a mile from the restaurant. From here it's a steady climb through the trees to the saddle above Williams Lake. You can ski down through the bowls surrounding the lake before heading back in a quick descent to the ski valley.

BULL-OF-THE-WOODS:
Class III   8 miles   Elevation: 9,500-11,500 feet

This is one of the most difficult cross-country routes I have ever skied, due to the steepness of the terrain. On any given weekend you'll meet the hearty expeditionary souls with skins or snowshoes journeying to Red River or Wheeler Peak. The recreational skier out for a day's leisurely skiing may not find Bull-of-the-Woods particularly recreational.

The trail begins at the east end of the Taos Ski Valley (where the road turns south to the private home area and Williams Lake Trail). A feasible day tour leads to Bull-of-the-Woods Pasture or on to Bull-of-the-Woods Mountain where a view to the northeast reveals the Red River Valley. The trail heads straight uphill to the east, on the north side of East Fork Rio Hondo and the south side of the powerline. Maintain an easterly course as the trail crosses several confusing powerline openings, until you reach the last pole. Here, cross the opening and you'll immediately see a red arrow on a tree pointing left. Follow the arrow and ascend a short hill, then follow the trail northeast as it again parallels the creek.

At a little over a mile the trail crosses a Forest Service road. Signs here indicate the junction of the Columbine-Twining National Recreation Trail to the left: Long Canyon Trail leads to Gold Hill, $4^1/_2$ miles, and to Columbine Campground, 13 miles. Long Canyon Trail can also be skied to a ridge above Goose Lake and back along Forest Trail 64 to Bull-of-the-Woods Trail, but is recommended only for advanced skiers.

Another sign in the middle of the forest road points out the continuation of Bull-of-the-Woods Trail to the pasture, to the northeast (right). Follow the arrow up through the trees to where the road turns north and climbs to another set of arrows on the trees. The arrow to the left points out a shortcut back to the ski valley; the arrow to the right points out the road switchback to the south. Follow the switchback to the right, and at the top of the hill you can see southwest over the ski valley to the Taos llano. The road then turns back northeast in a direct ascent to Bull-of-the-Woods Pasture at the top of the ridge.

If you choose to continue (if you have the stamina, that is) there are several possible routes here. Backpackers can follow the trail northeast to the West Fork Red River 6 miles down to New Mexico 150, which in turn leads to the village of Red River. To the south, Bull-of-the-Woods Trail continues up to the ridgeline where it junctions with Crest Ridge Trail #90, which in turn leads south around the west side of Bull-of-the-Woods Mountain. Backpackers can continue the 4 miles south to Wheeler Peak, and connect with the trail ascending Wheeler Peak from Williams Lake. (Snow conditions are usually poor here and preclude good ski touring.)

We once had an interesting experience near Bull-of-the-Woods Pasture, resting on the road, contemplating the last part of the climb. Gray jays had been following us up the trail from the creek. After throwing out a few cookie crumbs we realized how fearless these birds were, and my husband soon had them swooping down to take pieces of bread from his fingers. Next they began perching on his fingers to eat the bread in place. They followed us back down the mountain only as far as the Long Canyon Trail junction, then returned to their woodland home to await the next human invasion.

LONG CANYON-GOLD HILL:
Class III   9 miles   Elevation: 9,400-12,700 feet

This connecting route to Bull-of-the-Woods leads up into the high country above the Red River Valley. There is often danger of avalanche, so be sure to check with the Forest Service before skiing this tour.

Long Canyon trailhead begins about a mile up Bull-of-the-Woods Trail from the Taos Ski Valley (see Bull-of-the-Woods Trail description). A sign at the junction points north to Gold Hill, $4^1/2$ miles, and Columbine Campground, 13 miles. Follow the narrow Long Canyon Trail #63 to the northwest, along the east side of the creek. All along this route is evidence of the intense gold mining activities that took place in the late 19th and early 20th centuries.

At the north end of Long Canyon, about a mile in, follow the trail southeast as it switchbacks and climbs up the steep east slope of the canyon. The trail switchbacks up through the trees spread across this avalanche-prone slope. At the top of Long Canyon ridge the trail emerges into meadows with spectacular views of the Wheeler Peak high country behind you.

From here you can continue east to Gold Hill if the snow is stable. A steep traverse brings you to the panoramic views on top of Gold Hill. If you choose not to ski Gold Hill you might want to ski back to Bull-of-the-Woods Trail along an alternate route, Forest Trail #64, which follows the east ridge of Long Canyon. This trail intersects Long Canyon Trail in the saddle south of Goose Lake and meets up with Bull-of-the-Woods Trail at Bull-of-the-Woods Pasture.

Sangre de Cristo Mountains—Red River

The Red River area, like the Taos side of the Sangre de Cristos, provides excellent high-country skiing for the advanced skier, as well as offering more moderate tours for the intermediate skier (there are some beginner routes right out of town as well). You can reach Red River on New Mexico 38 east from Questa or north from Eagle Nest.

MALLETTE CANYON ROAD:
Class I 3 miles Elevation: 8,600-8,900 feet

Mallette Canyon Road begins one block west of the junction of NM 38 and Pioneer Road in the town of Red River. The route is a gentle ascent along Mallette Creek $1^1/2$ miles to the junction with Forest Road 597, which turns west to Sawmill Mountain (this route is designated Class III). Beginners can ski through the meadows at the junction before heading back to Red River.

PIONEER CANYON ROAD:
Class III 7 miles Elevation: 8,600-10,000 feet

This combination road-Forest Trail 64 heads west to Pioneer

Lake from the Red River Ski Area. You can ski to the old Caribel Mine where the ore-processing mill is still standing. The trail continues along Pioneer Creek to the lake.

ENCHANTED FOREST CROSS-COUNTRY SKI AREA:
Class I-II   19 miles of trail   Elevation: 9,800-10,300 feet

Located on NM 38 at Bobcat Pass, this popular, private ski area provides a series of groomed trails, signed and accompanied by a detailed map. There are numerous trails appropriate for the beginner skier, while the intermediate skier can ski to the cabins and outer loops that provide panoramic views of the high Wheeler Peak Wilderness. The area is owned by the Miller family, who also own Miller's Crossing in the town of Red River, where you can purchase tickets, rent skis, or sign up for lessons. Call (505) 754-2374 for information.

GOOSE LAKE, FOREST TRAIL 66:
Class III   16 miles   Elevation: 8,600-11,600 feet

This trail begins .7 miles south of the junction of NM 38 and New Mexico 150 on 150 (this paved road terminates about 7 miles south). You can avoid the steep first part of the trail by taking the chairlift to the top of the ski area. The trail leads to the high country at Goose Lake (8 miles) and connects with all the trails coming from the Taos Ski Valley side of the mountains.

EAST FORK RIVER TRAIL 56:
Class II-III   6.5 miles   Elevation: 9,400-11,500 feet

Follow NM 150 south to the end of the pavement (6.7 miles) to a sign which indicates the East Fork Trail to the left, across a bridge. The road heads south through a summer home area (and through two gates) to a primitive road where the wilderness gateway sign is. Because of it's exposure, the road is often crusty or icy, and is also used by snowmobilers. At the wilderness sign snow conditions generally improve as the trail enters the forest canopy. A practice area can be found across the river to the west.

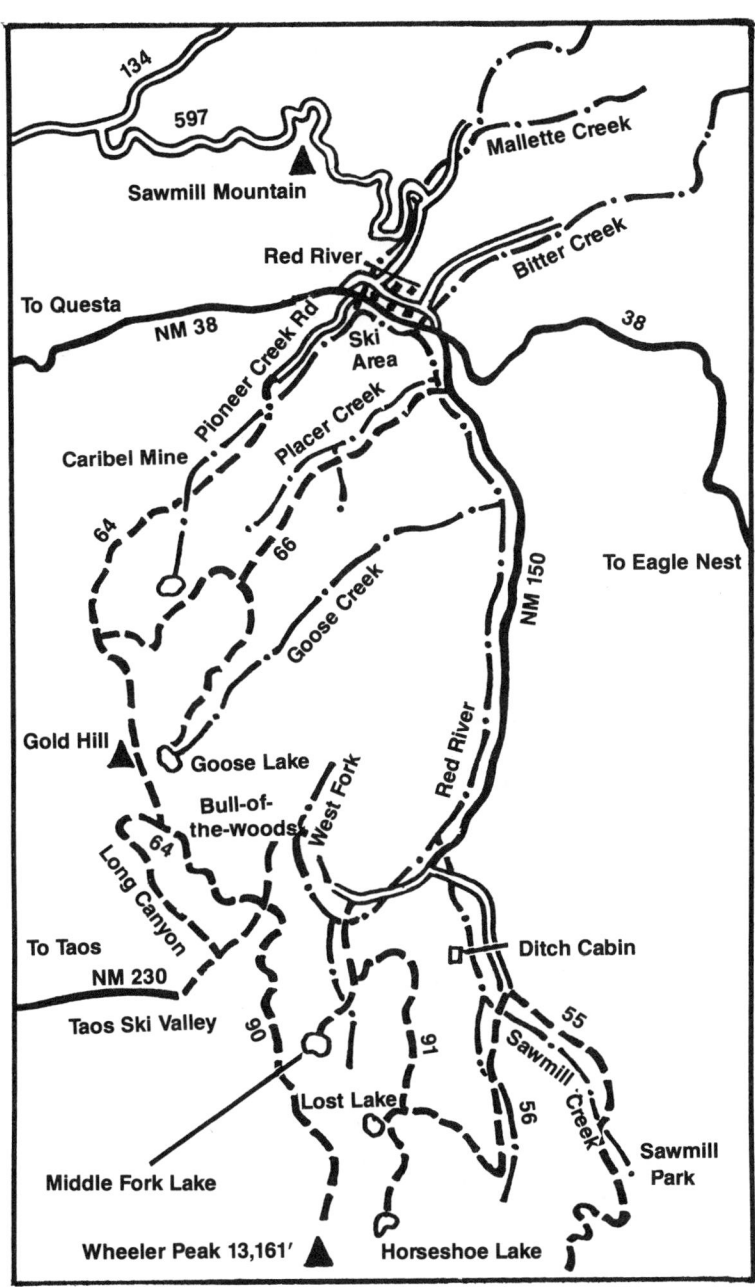

RED RIVER AREA

Its a one-half mile climb to the Ditch Cabin site (an abandoned mining project, where the Elizabeth Ditch once ran to Eagle Nest) where the road narrows to a trail. From here the trail travels south on the east side of the East Fork in a gentle ascent for 1 mile to the junction with Sawmill Park Trail #55. East Fork River Trail continues south along the river (which is quite a ways down in the canyon).

The trail gradually climbs over a distance of 6 miles to either Horseshoe Lake or Lost Lake, which is about as far as you will get in a day tour. At Lost Lake is the junction of East Fork Trail with Lost Lake Trail, connecting to Middle Fork Lake Trail. The downhill part of the tour can be difficult to negotiate on the sometimes narrow trail unless snow conditions are good.

WEST FORK TRAIL 58:
Class II-III   8 miles   Elevation: 9,400-10,200 feet

You can ski along the West Fork Red River, Forest Trail #58, all the way to Bull-of-the-Woods Pasture on the west side of the mountains, or stay on the Red River side for an easier tour along the river. West Fork Road begins at the end of the pavement along NM 150 (6.7 miles south from NM 38) and heads southwest along the river.

Follow the road west along the north side of Red River in a gentle tour through exposed terrain (the road may be quite crusty due to its exposure), past the summer parking area. At about 1 mile a gate indicates the junction of Middle Fork Trail, which turns south and climbs to Middle Fork Lake.

Continue west beyond the gate as the road follows the west fork of Red River in a steeper ascent. The less experienced skier won't want to ski much more than a mile along this route, as the terrain becomes quite steep where it leaves the power line and winds around to the northwest (right). Views of the valley open up behind you.

The road narrows to a trail and bears left, towards the river. This last section of trail, on the south side of the river, climbs to the power easement and on to Bull-of-the-Woods in a steep climb that only the most advanced skier wants to attempt. At Bull-of-the-Woods Pasture Middle Fork River Trail meets Bull-of-the-Woods Trail ascending from the Taos Ski Valley, and Crest Ridge Trail, which continues south to Wheeler Peak.

MIDDLE FORK LAKE TRAIL 140:
Class III   6 miles   Elevation: 9,400-10,800 feet :

Take the West Fork Red River Road at the end of the pavement on NM 150 southwest, as you did in the previous section, to the junction of Middle Fork Lake Trail #140 (about 1 mile).

Cross the river and head south along this middle fork of the river. The trail climbs steeply to a series of switchbacks, which bear southeast, and are easier to ski than the initial climb through the trees. At mile 1 is the junction of the Lost Lake Trail #91, leading to Lost Lake, 4 miles to the southeast (left).

Continue to the southwest towards Middle Fork Lake. Just beyond the junction Middle Fork Trail crosses a waterfall and climbs more steeply to the lake, which sits in a basin below the 12,000 foot peaks to the southwest (Frazier Mountain is directly across the lake). I once skied this trail in a snowstorm that provided fresh, powdery snow, and it was one of the most exhilarating downhill runs I've ever made. If the snow is old and crusty the downhill part of the tour can be treacherous.

Sangre de Cristo Mountains—Taos Canyon

Most of the ski tours in the Taos Canyon area are appropriate for beginners; several of these areas have been closed to snowmobiles by the Forest Service to provide safe ski touring. I have listed the various areas, starting west to east, and the corresponding mileage from Taos.

MONDRAGON CANYON: 9.8 miles
Class I-II   16 miles   Elevation: 8,200-9,600 feet

This area is reserved for cross-country skiers and offers varied terrain and expansive vistas of the Taos Valley. The trailhead is on the south side of the road where a locked gate indicates the forest road. There is a parking pull-off on the north side of the highway.

The road heads southwest in a steady climb to the east side of Mondragon Canyon. This lower portion of the road deteriorates quickly due to its open exposure, so it's best to ski the area after a snow storm.

After several miles, the trail reaches some birms in the road and turns west, across the creek. It continues climbing in the high country aspens, circling around to the east as views of the Taos llano open up. The trail continues climbing as it works its way southwest to the ridge of the Fernando Mountains near Suazo Canyon.

GARCIA PARK   BORREGO CROSSING. 13 miles
Class I-II   14 miles   Elevation: 8,400-10,000 feet

Access to Garcia Park is Forest Road 437 at the Valle Escondido junction. Park here and ski south the 7 miles to Garcia Park along this obvious forest road. The first part of the road detours to the west around Mascareñas Canyon, then continues south again. There may be patches of bare road here before the trail climbs to views of Wheeler Peak and Palo Flechado Pass (at the east end of U.S. 64 and NM 38). The road continues south to the junction with Garcia Park, one mile to the east (the continuation of FR 437) and Sierra de Don Fernando, 2 miles west (Forest Road 445). At Garcia Park the terrain opens up into beautiful meadows. Forest Road 437 continues south to Borrego Crossing.

Several trails also begin at the Valle Escondido junction—Trail 437A and 436B—leading southeast 6 miles to Garcia Park, but are open to snowmobiles.

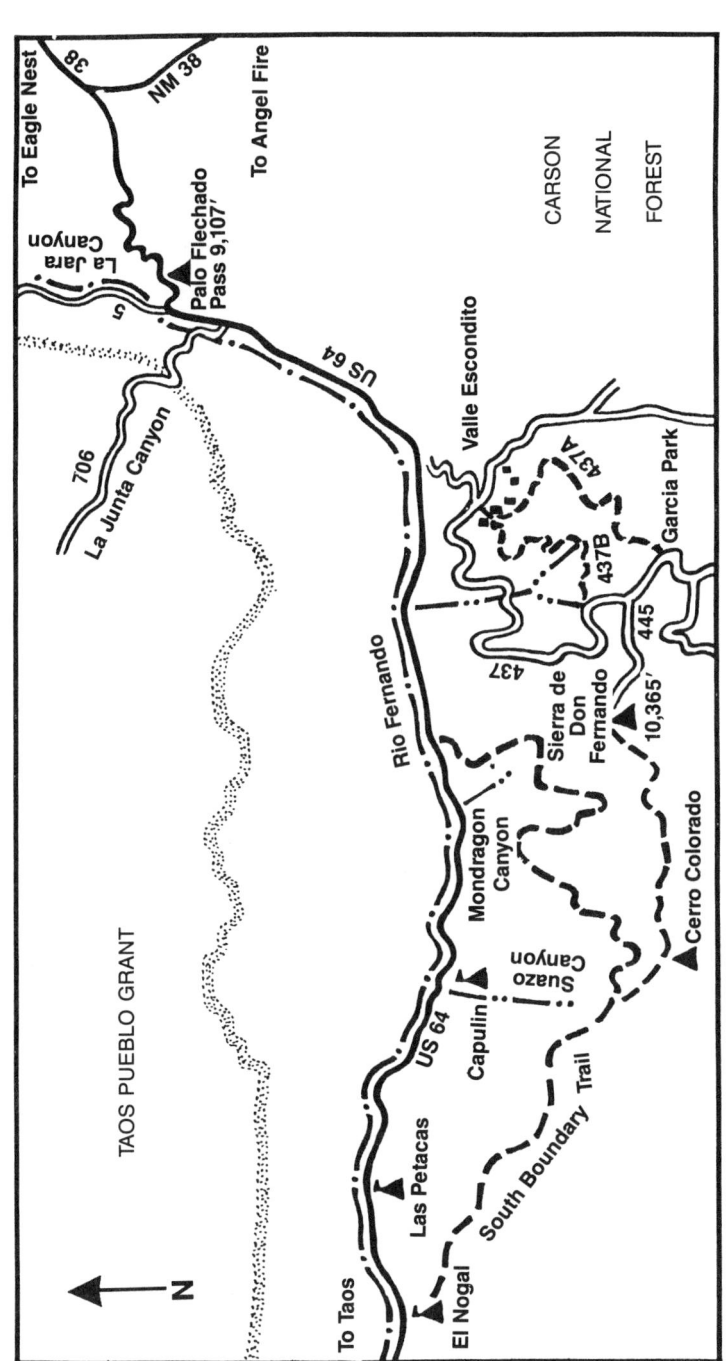

TAOS CANYON

SIERRA de DON FERNANDO—SOUTH BOUNDARY TRAIL 164: 13 miles
Class III   30 miles   Elevation: 8,400-10,365 feet

This advanced ski trail leads 15 miles west from Sierra de Don Fernando off FR 437 to El Nogal Campground (3 miles east of Taos on U.S. 64). At the junction of Forest roads 445 and 437 near Garcia Park ski west about 1 1/2 miles to Sierra de Don Fernando Peak, 10,365 feet high. This peak provides a 360 degree view of Wheeler Peak to the north and the Pecos Wilderness south. This trail can be followed all the way west to a junction with the Mondragon Canyon Trail and on to El Nogal Campground. It can be difficult to follow, however, and contains many hard climbs and descents.

LA JUNTA CANYON, FOREST ROAD 706: 16 miles
Class I   6 miles   Elevation: 8,700-9,200 feet

This easy forest road heads north off U.S. 64 to the boundary of the Taos Pueblo Grant. The wide canyon road climbs in a gentle ascent through meadows to the boundary ridge. Because of its southern exposure, the season here may be short.

LA JARA CANYON, FOREST ROAD 5: 17 miles
Class I   4 miles   Elevation: 8,900-9,200 feet

Perfect for the beginner, Forest Road 5 through La Jara Canyon also travels north to the Taos Pueblo Grant boundary. The road follows a stream through white fir vegetation and meadows, and numerous side roads offer tour detours throughout the canyon.

Sangre de Cristo Mountains—U.S. Hill

U.S. Hill on the east of Taos provides some of the best beginner and intermediate ski touring in the Carson. This ski tour area is accessed via NM 518 (the highway to Mora) east from Taos, or NM 75 north from Peñasco.

U.S. HILL—GALLEGOS PEAK:
Class I-II   12 miles   Elevation: 8,500-10,000 feet

The trailhead is located on the north side of NM 518, 12 miles east of Ranchos de Taos and 3.3 miles northwest of NM 75, the highway to Peñasco. Gallegos Peak Road, Forest Road 442, leads 12 miles to Gallegos Peak and is used extensively by snowmobilers. But there is now a cross-country ski route bypass that leads northeast from the junction of 442 and the highway, recrosses the forest road a mile later, and ties in with the Amole Canyon system of three looped trails to the south. From where the cross-country route recrosses FR 442 you can continue along the road to Gallegos Peak.

PICURIS PEAK, FOREST ROAD 114:
Class II   16 miles   Elevation: 8,500-10,800 feet

This trailhead is located on the south side of the NM 518, 12.8 miles east of Ranchos de Taos and 3.3 miles west of the junction of NM 75 leading to Peñasco. The road is supposedly closed to snowmobiles beyond the meadow adjacent to the highway, and leads 8 miles to Picuris Peak. The first 3 miles are a gentle ascent, with rolling terrain. The road then steepens a little as it junctions with Road 469 from Vadito, winds around the north side of the peak, and then climbs the steeper west side to the top. There, the views of the Peñasco Valley and Truchas Peaks are magnificent. Snow conditions vary according to exposure.

A 6-mile tour can be made to the Camino Real, the oldest road in the United States. Past the meadow the trail enters ponderosa pine and ascends several steep hills until it levels out as it circles the south side of the peak. Views to the southwest open up—Jicarita Peak to the Truchas Peaks and on to the Jemez Mountains. The terrain is rolling here, and makes for an easy tour to a sign indicating the Camino Real at Osha Canyon.

AMOLE CANYON:
Class I-III   Variable mileage   Elevation 8,100-9,000 feet

This system of three loop trails follows old logging roads between NM 518 and Ojito Maes. The trailhead is 14.6 miles east of Ranchos de Taos and 1.6 miles from the junction of NM 75 leading to Peñasco. Amole Loop is a beginner trail that heads north from FR 703 a quarter mile from NM 518, circles east, returns to the road, then loops south in a 3.1-mile tour. The Lower Loop, rated Class II or III, is 6.1 miles in length and follows Amole Canyon northeast to the Upper Loop. This trail, 7.2 miles in length and rated Class II or III, loops around to the north, intersects with Forest Road 442 from U.S. Hill, then reconnects with the Lower Loop. A one-way system of markers allows you to ski any single loop or combination, eventually guiding you back to NM 518.

AMOLE LOOP: *3.1 miles*

Follow FR 703 from the parking area on NM 518 about one-quarter mile to the sign on the left that marks the trailhead. The trails hugs the trees on the west side of the clearing, then crosses the creek and heads north up the ridge. At the top the trail divides: the easier route turns east (right) and follows the top of the ridge in a level tour; the alternate route follows the black diamond trail down the backside of the ridge in a nice run down into a drainage. The trail then turns east up the creek and ties in with the Upper-Lower Loop trails. Turn south and follow the arrows back up the ridge. You'll pass the junction of the easier ridgetop route, then quickly return to FR 703. Because of the exposure in the creek drainages this part of the trail can quickly deteriorate in sunny, warm conditions.

Once back at the road follow it south past the Upper and Lower Loop turn-offs to the end of the road where it becomes a trail (another unblazed route continues east). The trail skirts the edge of a large meadow. After a short, downhill glide the trail turns west and divides; a short, easy route heads north across the meadow towards the road; the outer loop continues west in an up

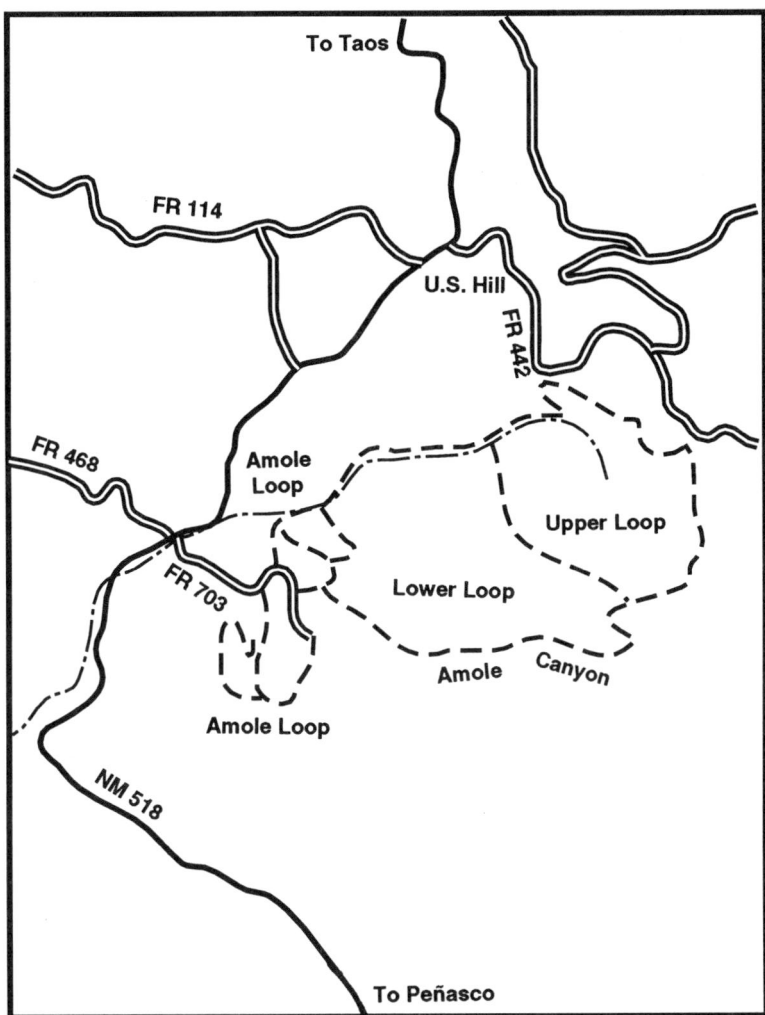

AMOLE CANYON

and down glide through the trees. It passes the intersection of the easier route in the meadow just before it returns to the road at the outhouse. This route is also quite exposed and can quickly become icy in sunny conditions.

LOWER LOOP: *6.1 miles*

The Lower and Upper loops both begin as one trail about a half mile from the highway. It's a steady uphill climb to an arrow on a tree which is rather deceptive. The arrow looks like it's pointing south, but in actuality the trail continues straight ahead, up Amole Canyon (the trail to your left is the returning Lower-Upper loop trail) The trail continues climbing through ponderosa pine vegetation into spruce-fir country. The climb is fairly easy until the trail turns in a more northerly direction towards the head of the canyon. At a sharp turn to the left, the trail levels out, circling the ridge. A great view of the Jemez Mountains is visible to the west. Continue a short distance around the ridge to the junction with the Upper Loop Trail, which continues straight ahead. Lower Loop trail turns northwest at the warning sign which says the next quarter-mile section is for the expert skier only. While this section is quite steep, if skied with caution an intermediate skier is quite capable of enjoying its long, downhill glide. The descent levels out into a nice glide down through the trees to the junction with the returning Upper Loop Trail in a large drainage. A hill to the east provides a good telemark practice area. An arrow on a tree indicates the continuation of the Lower-Upper Loop trails down the creek to the west. There may be snowmobile tracks throughout this area, so watch for the trail as it turns southwest back into the trees. At the next clearing the trail turns sharply left at the junction with Amole Loop Trail, where the trails converge and ascend the short hill to a glide back down to the Lower-Upper Loop trails' origin just above the forest road.

UPPER LOOP: *7.2 miles*

At the black diamond indicating the return of Lower Loop Trail, continue northeast along the Upper Loop as it circles the ridge in a level tour. The route soon turns north and follows an old logging road in a gentle descent. Follow the blue blazes as the route leaves the road and turns northwest in a fast glide through the trees to a second logging road, where it levels out again. Follow this road to a fenceline, where the trail turns left, into the trees again, for another fast run. This short run brings you to the junction with FR 422, which originates to the west at NM 518. A sign indicates the Upper Loop Trail heads south, down through the clearing, bearing left, into the trees. The trail emerges in a creek drainage; make a sharp turn to the west (right), down the creek, and follow the blazes along the south side of the creek to the junction with Lower Loop Trail, which continues west back to FR 703.

Sangre de Cristo Mountains—Peñasco

SANTA BARBARA CAMPGROUND ROAD:
Class I   6 miles   Elevation: 8,400-8,860 feet

Forest Road 116 leading to Santa Barbara Campground provides excellent skiing for the beginner, and Forest Trail 24, from the campground into the Pecos Wilderness, offers high-country ski touring for more advanced skiers.

Drive to Peñasco along NM 68 to NM 75 from Española or NM 518 to NM 75 from Taos. At the junction of NM 75 and NM 73 in Peñasco, take 73 southeast (the only way it goes) $1^1/2$ miles to the junction with FR 116. It's 3 miles along 116 to the turnoff to Hodges Campground, which marks the forest boundary, and 3 miles from the boundary to Santa Barbara Campground. The road to the forest boundary is usually kept open; drive as far as you can until there is adequate snow for skiing.

The road follows the Rio Santa Barbara on the right, past beautiful meadows and stands of aspen. The forest road down to Hodges Campground descends to the river and parallels FR 116, providing nice campsites on the river bank. After a mile-and-a-half climb along 116 you reach the second Hodges Campground entrance to the right, and 116 then crosses the Rio Santa Barbara. Now the river is on your left, carving a steep canyon through the aspen and spruce-fir forest. Jicarita Peak looms snow covered ahead of you. The road continues its ascent another mile and a half to the campground.

Middle Fork Trail #24 takes off to the right at the east end of the campground loop. The trail climbs gently to the southeast, following the Rio Santa Barbara 2 miles to the junction with West Fork Trail #25. Both trails follow the two forks of the river high into the Pecos Wilderness, and provide a beautiful but arduous ski tour for the more advanced skier. Beginners can stay on Forest Road 116 as it loops through the campground and returns to Peñasco in a gentle cross-country glide down the river valley.

Sangre de Cristo Mountains—Tres Ritos

This area on NM 518 south of NM 75 offers varied terrain for all ski levels. I have listed the ski areas from the west to the east with their various mileages from the junction of NM 518 and NM 75.

AGUA PIEDRA CAMPGROUND, TRAIL 19: 7 miles
Class I-II   4 miles   Elevation: 8,400-9,200 feet

This snowplay area provides open terrain for beginners to practice their cross-country ski technique, with a shelter area and parking facilities. More advanced skiers can follow Agua Piedra Trail #19 south to the Knob and on to Angostura Trail #89, or turn southeast on Comales Trail #22 to North Fork Trail #36 toward Jicarita Peak.

Park your car at the gate marking the entrance to the shelter. Follow the road south through the trees into a large meadow and across the meadow to the trailhead. Once through the gate, the trail follows Agua Piedra Creek in a gentle ascent. The first half mile is on the east side of the creek; once you cross over to the west side, the trail becomes a little harder to follow as it meanders along the creek, crossing several more times. Watch for old blazes on the trees. At 2 miles, the trail divides; Agua Piedra Trail #19 (called Serpent Lake Trail on the sign) continues southeast to the

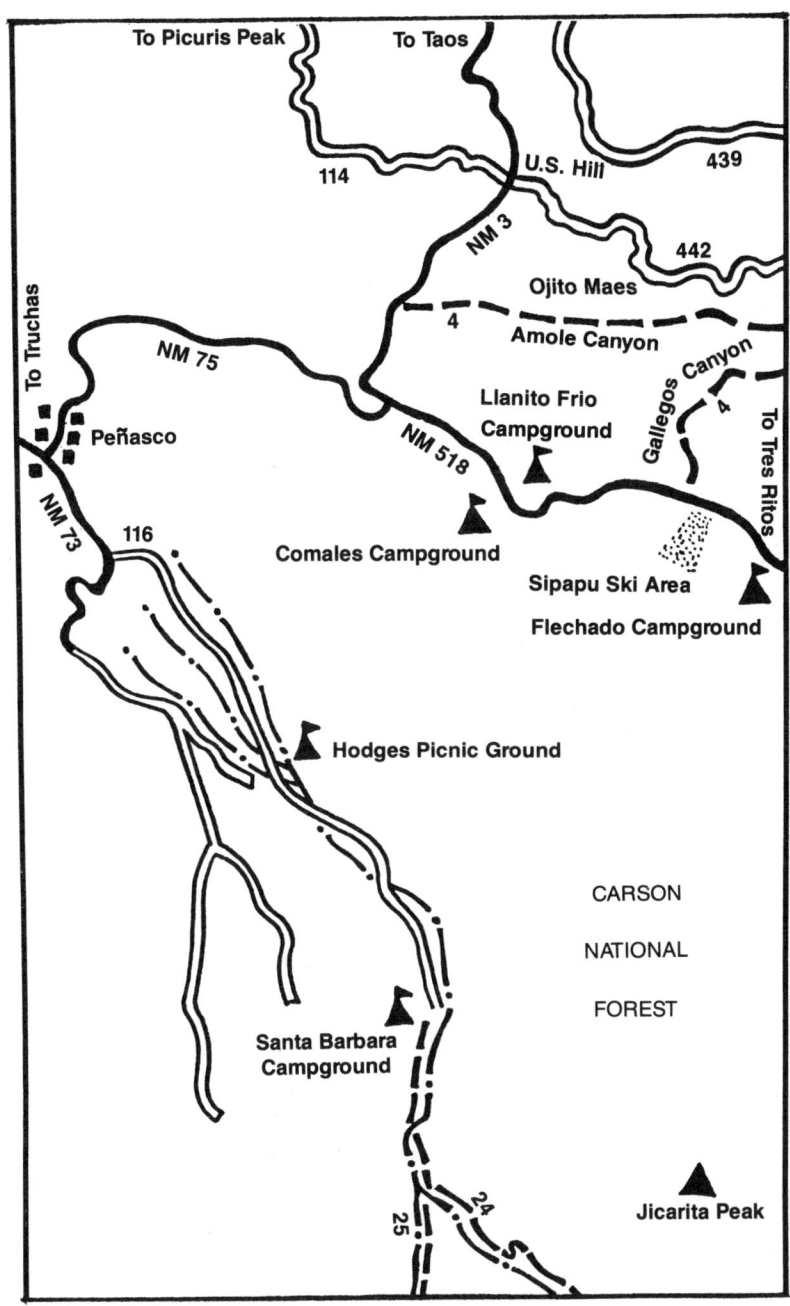

SANTA BARBARA CAMPGROUND

Knob and on to Serpent Lake. Comales Trail #22 (called Ripley's Point Trail on the sign) turns southwest and leads to North Fork Trail #36 and Jicarita Peak in a steep climb, recommended for only advanced skiers. For those skiers who want to ski further on Agua Piedra Trail #19, a route that begins at Angostura Campground and ends at Agua Piedra Campground is described in the following Angostura-Agua Piedra Trails section.

LA JUNTA CANYON—DURAN CANYON: 9 miles
Class I-II   4-8 miles   Elevation: 8,600-10,000 feet

In a good snow year this forest road is not traveled by vehicles and makes a nice cross-country tour to Duran Canyon Campground (2 miles) and on up to La Junta Campground (4 miles). You can also ski up Duran Canyon east from the campground toward Romero Lake, a more difficult route. If snow conditions are not adequate below La Junta Campground, drive farther up the road and ski into the high country.

ANGOSTURA CANYON TRAIL 89: 10.6 miles
Class I-III   2-6 miles   Elevation: 8,800-10,000 feet

Located just southeast of Tres Ritos on NM 518, this trail can be skied by both beginners and more experienced skiers venturing as far as their ability allows. The first part of the trail, through the campground and summer home area, is an easy 2-mile round-trip, while the continuation of Angostura Trail to FR 161 provides a steeper, narrow climb into the high country.

Located on the south side of the highway, there is no sign visible from the highway, so watch carefully for the campground turnoff.

Ski the campground road southeast to a sign indicating a summer home area. It's a gentle ascent to the gate of the home area, past the Tres Ritos Boy Scout Camp. There are several beautiful cabins tucked away in the trees, accessible by vehicle only in the summertime. At the "dead end" sign the road narrows to a trail, which soon crosses Angostura Creek. Beginners can turn back here to complete the 2-mile round-trip.

The trail continues a short distance along the west side of Angostura Creek to the junction of FT 9A heading northwest, a short-cut to Agua Piedra Trail #19. Angostura Trail continues up Angostura Canyon. It's a moderate climb up the canyon along the

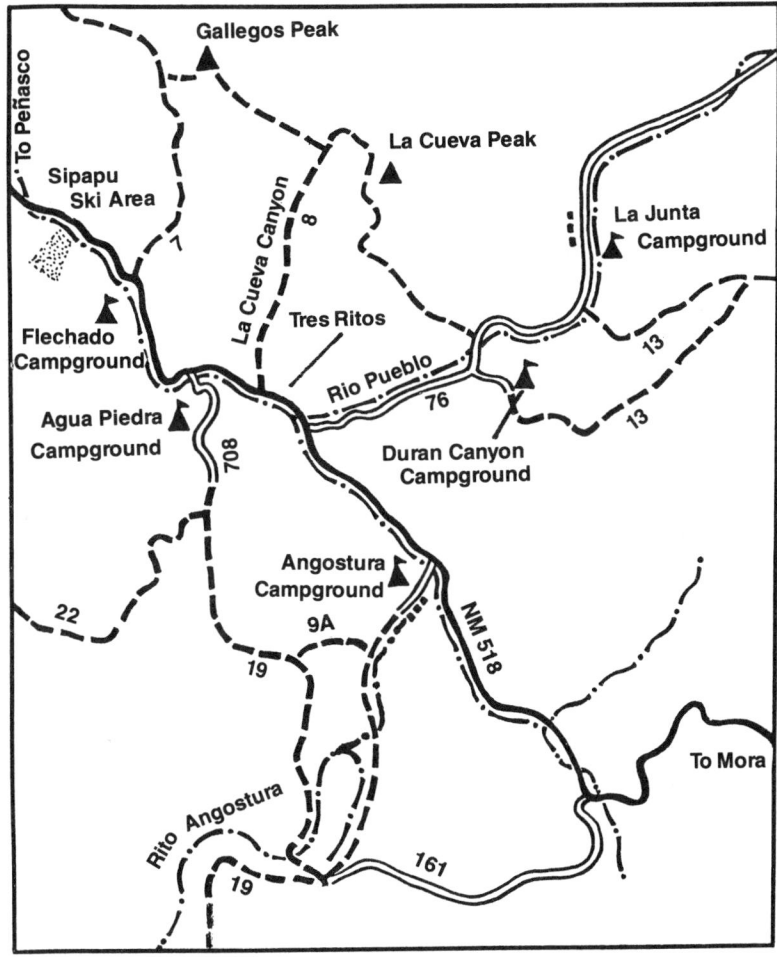

TRES RITOS AREA: LA JUNTA CANYON—DURAN CANYON; ANGOSTURA-AQUA PIEDRA

Meadow below the Knob

west side of the creek. At about 2 miles, the trail enters a meadow where the scrapped, wooden remnants of the Santa Barbara Tie and Pole Company lie heaped under the snow. The trail leaves the Angostura drainage and continues to the junction with Forest Road 161. Only experienced skiers should attempt this 6-mile round trip.

ANGOSTURA-AGUA PIEDRA TRAILS: 10.6 miles
Class III   6 miles   Elevation: 8,800-10,000 feet

One of my favorite ski tours, this trip requires leaving a car at Agua Piedra Campground (7 miles from the junction with NM 75 to Peñasco) and a car at Angostura Campground where the tour begins.

Ski up through the summer home area and beyond the "Dead End" sign where the road becomes a trail. Once you cross the creek, look for Forest Trail 9A which turns sharply right, to the northwest. The trail climbs quite steeply for a short distance above the canyon, and then levels out. At about 3/4 mile you'll reach a beautiful meadow where you can see the bare Jicarita Peak ridge to the west. Snowmobiles do frequent this meadow, so it's best to do the tour on a weekday, if you can.

A sign in the meadow indicates the junction with Agua Piedra Trail #19, which leads south (left) to FR 161 and Serpent Lake, and north (right) to the Knob, the high point of the tour, and on to Agua Piedra Campground. You can ski for about a mile south along FT #19 before the route narrows and becomes too hard to follow in the snow.

Our route continues north. Cross the meadow (there's a blue arrow on the back of the sign indicating the way) and into the aspen trees which mark the route. We usually put our climbing skins on here, as the climb to the Knob is steep.

Watch for old blazes on the trees as you ascend to a meadow where the trail momentarily levels out, then enters the trees again in a steady climb to the Knob, the hill on your right. At the top of the climb you'll reach another small meadow, where a spur trail heads up the Knob and the gate through the fence indicates the trail down the north side of the canyon to Agua Piedra. It's the perfect spot for lunch.

The first quarter mile of the descent to the Agua Piedra is quite steep down a narrow, twisty trail. If the snow is hard-pack you might want to keep your skins on until the trail levels out at the creek. If the trail is unbroken through powder (as it usually is) you can negotiate the trail without skins. Again, carefully watch for old blazes as the trail is not that obvious.

When you reach Agua Piedra Creek the terrain becomes less steep and the trail follows the west side of the creek in a fun glide down the canyon. There's a trail sign at the junction with Comales Trail #22 (the sign says Ripley's Point Trail) which leads west to North Fork Trail #36; it's 2 more miles north along #19 to Agua Piedra Campground. This last part of the trail is a gentle descent along the creek (it crosses the creek several times) to a meadow which leads to the campground road.

Sangre de Cristo Mountains—Brazos Area

US Highway 64 between Tres Piedras and Tierra Amarilla is not consistently plowed during the winter months, but you can often make it to the Hopewell Lake area from either side. Check with the Tres Piedras Ranger District for highway conditions. If you are able to access the area you'll find open meadows and many forest roads suitable for skiing. If you take a vehicle into the area be sure that it is well equipped for heavy snow conditions. The State Highway Department is not responsible for stranded vehicles. The area is also open to snowmobiles, so use caution. Several trails and mileages from Tres Piedras are listed below.

BISCARA TRAIL, FR 421: 11.8 miles
Class I   Variable mileage   Elevation: 8,900 feet

This forest road leads north up Cañada Biscara in a motor travel restricted area and ties in with many other forest roads. There is some snowmobile traffic in the area.

MAQUINITA CANYON: 14 miles
Class II   2½-5 miles   Elevation: 8,600-9,400 feet

This system of trails has been laid out and marked by the Forest Service and consists of a series of 5 routes that lie between

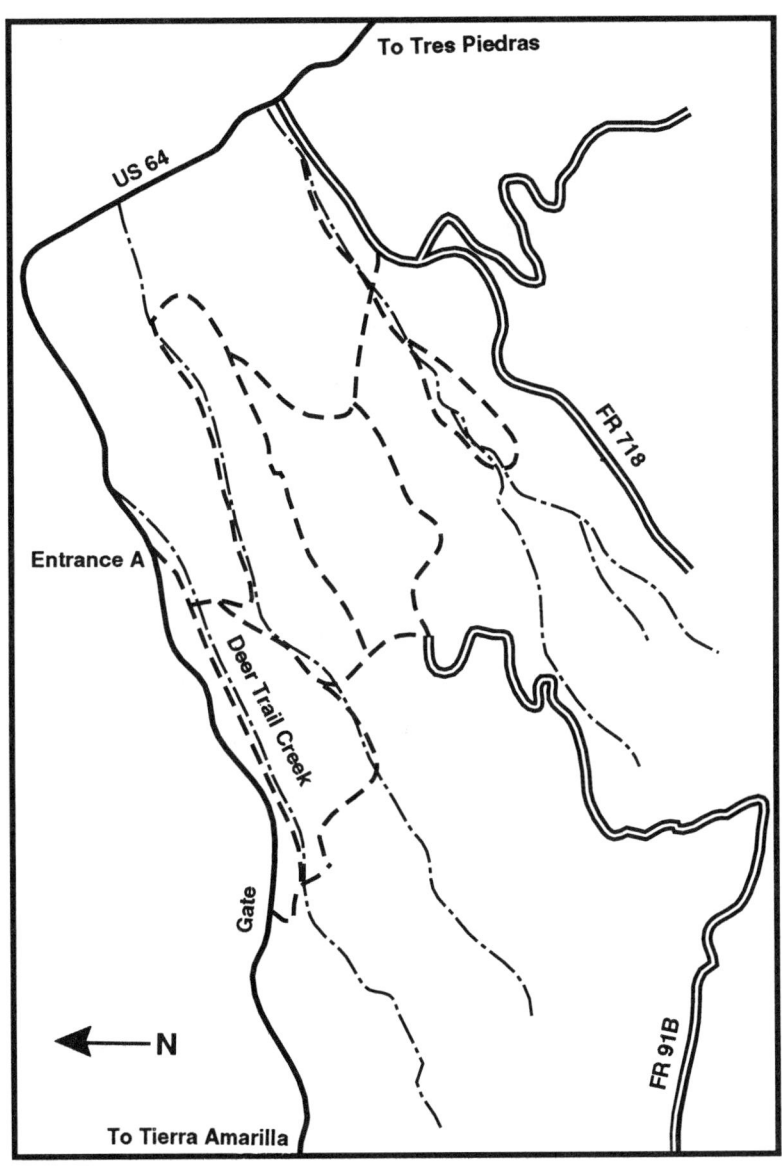

MAQUINITA CANYON

Maquinita Canyon and Deer Trail Canyon. They can be accessed from the Maquinita Canyon trailhead or several other entrances further along US 64. The routes provide fairly easy terrain through aspen meadows, as well as access to the Burned Mountain area for more advanced skiers.

At the Maquinita Canyon trailhead Routes 3,4,5, and 6 are accessed. Park alongside the road where the sign with a skier marks the trailhead. The route heads south, up Maquinita Canyon. Just after the canyon sign the routes divide: the route to the left follows FR 718 up into the trees; the route to the right follows the fence line directly up Maquinita Canyon. Both routes reunite about one half mile later in the canyon; a sign here indicates the junction of Routes 5 and 6, which turn west, up the ridge. It's easy to miss this turn, as tracks usually lead straight up Maquinita Canyon to Route 4, an alternate $2^1/_2$-mile route that loops up through the trees at the head of the canyon.

To reach the inner loops, 5 and 6, turn sharply up the canyon, just past the sign, until you see an arrow in a clearing guiding you up the ridge. Climb west, up the ridge, to a meadow; cross the meadow until you see the next arrow guiding you back into the trees. At the next sign the routes divide: Route 6 continues down the hill to Amos Tank; Route 5 turns south and climbs along the top of the ridge. You can ski either way to make a loop and return to Maquinita Canyon. Route 5 continues along the ridgetop, affording periodic views of Wheeler Peak to the northeast, then descends into the next drainage, where you can turn downhill (this is actually part of Route 2, accessed from Deer Trail Canyon), and meet Route 6 at Amos Tank. Return via Route 6 to Maquinita Canyon.

Several more loops can be skied in the next drainages northwest, towards Deer Trail Canyon. At the junction of Route 5 and Route 2, in the Amos Tank drainage, you can ski north, across the ridge, to the next drainage. If you turn right, down the drainage, you can ski a loop which follows the drainage towards the highway, then circles back to the junction of Route 6 at Amos Tank. If

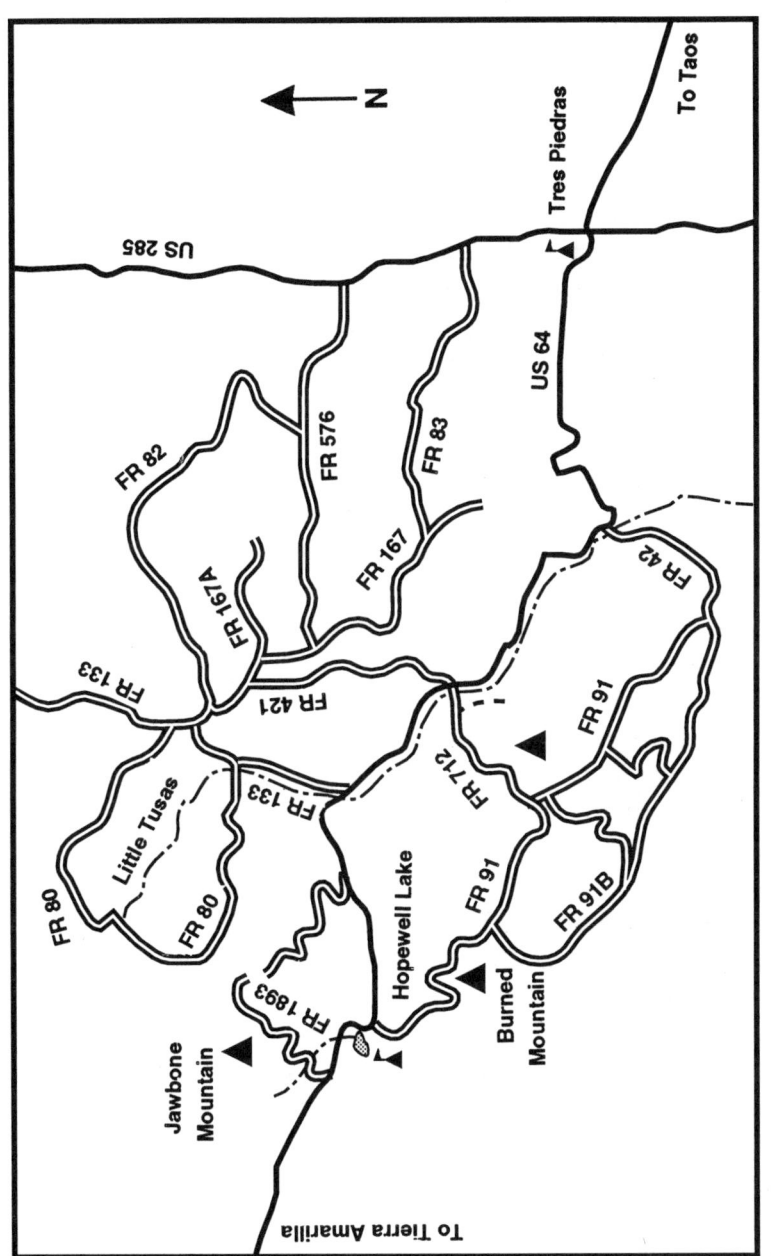

BRAZOS AREA

you turn left, up the drainage, you can follow Route 5 as it turns north, across the ridge, to the gate on US 64 at Deer Trail Bowl. Route 1 originates here, and travels along Deer Trail Creek, paralleling the highway east to Entrance A on US 64. Just before the highway intersection Route 1 turns south and accesses the inner loops between Deer Trail Canyon and Maquinita Canyon.

LITTLE TUSAS CREEK, FR 133: 14.8 miles
Class I-II   Variable mileage   Elevation: 8,780-9,200 feet

This forest road leads north several miles to FR 80 and on to Cisneros Park (5 miles), providing open, easy terrain for skiing.

DEER TRAIL CANYON, ENTRANCE A: 16.2 miles
Class II   2½-5 miles   9,400-8,400 feet

This is another entrance to the Maquinita Canyon area, accessing Routes 1, 2 and 6, as described in the Maquinita Canyon section. A Forest Service sign with a trail map is posted on the south side of the highway marking the trailhead.

FOREST ROAD 795: 16.7 miles
Class I-II   12 miles   Elevation: 9,000 feet

This gently rolling forest road through a motor travel restricted area leads north to Duran Canyon and offers beginner to intermediate skiing terrain. There is little snowmobile use.

ENTRANCE, ROUTE 5: 17.2 miles

This is where Route 5 begins, on the south side of the highway, tying in with Routes 1, 2 and 6.

BURNED MOUNTAIN, FR 91B: 22 miles
Class I-II   Variable mileage   Elevation: 9,760-10,000 feet

This forest road ski trail is accessed at the Hopewell Lake Campground turnoff, where a small parking area is plowed. The trail travels southeast to Burned Mountain, offering easy glides and long vistas.

FOREST ROADS 1892, 1893: 24 miles
Class I-II Variable mileage Elevation: 9,800-10,200 feet

These roads lead north to the Placer Creek Meadows, an area appropriate for beginner skiers, and on to Jawbone Mountain, through the Placer Mine area. This tour provides views of the spectacular Brazos Cliffs, and telemarkers will find hills to practice their skills. You may have to park at the Hopewell Lake turn-off and ski the several miles to these forest roads, as US 64 is seldom plowed beyond Hopewell.

Sangre de Cristo Mountains—Valle Vidal Unit

This northern-most district of Carson National Forest was acquired by the Forest Service from Penzoil Corporation, whose lands were originally part of Vermejo Park. The area has a rich and colorful history, from its original land grant status to its days as a playground for the rich. Although extensively logged and mined, the 100,000 acre Valle Vidal Unit is currently managed with an emphasis on wildlife habitat—huge herds of elk graze its vast meadows and wooded hills. Much of the area is closed to use during elk calving season, but winter use coincides with the movement of elk to the east-side winter range.

Access to the Valle Vidal is east from the town of Questa via NM 196 and FR 1950, and west from the town of Cimarron via US 64 and FR 1950. Because of its open, rolling terrain (elevations vary from about 8,000 to 10,000 feet), the area is ideally suited for cross-country skiing. However, due to the distances from the access towns (17 miles from Questa and 27 miles from Cimarron) and the fact that FR 1950 is unplowed, the area remains remote and little used. The Forest Service has restricted snowmobile use to the south side of FR 1950, while cross-country skiing is permitted on the north side. The following ski route is recommended by the Forest Service; be sure to check at district headquarters in Questa for snow conditions and status of the roads.

POWDERHOUSE-LITTLE COSTILLA PEAK TRAIL:
Class II-III   Variable mileage   Elevation: 9,000-12,000 feet

This route can be accessed from Costilla, near the Valle Vidal boundary, to which the road is usually plowed. At the junction of FR 1950 and Forest Road 1900, ski north from Comanche Point to the signed trailhead on the east side of the road. The trail leads 10 miles to Little Costilla Peak, at 12,584 feet in elevation the tallest mountain in the Valle Vidal. The trail continues southeast another 10 miles to its eastern trailhead on FR 1950 (3 miles south of Comanche Point). You can ski as far as you like, then return to Comanche Point.

CARSON AND RIO GRANDE NATIONAL FORESTS

San Juan Mountains

Many of the ski tours in the Chama area are actually in Colorado, just over the New Mexico line, with a departure from Colorado 17 north from Chama to Antonito, Colorado. This is the route of the famous Cumbres and Toltec Scenic Railroad, whose narrow-gauge tracks and Cumbres Pass Station are visible from the ski trails. Snow conditions are usually the best in the state, and the terrain is spectacular. Unfortunately, there has always existed a conflict between cross-country skiers and snowmobilers, and the Forest Service is now attempting to reduce the friction by separating the two activities on a volunteer basis. Most of the trails listed below are recommended for cross-country skiers, although snowmobiles still frequent the area. I have listed the mileages to the trailheads along CO 17 north from the junction of NM 17 and US 84 (to Pagosa Springs) in Chama.

LOBO LODGE ROAD: 6.6 miles
Class I   12 miles   Elevation: 8,400-8,600 feet

This tour along Lobo Lodge Road begins in New Mexico and leads 6 miles through private land to the Rio Grande National Forest of Colorado; a Forest Service sign says "Chama River, Rio Grande National Forest" at the trailhead. Turn left (west) onto the unmaintained road and park. The Lobo Lodge cabins sit just to the south of the road, which heads west across private property in a very moderate climb. As the road turns north the first view of the high Colorado peaks of the San Juan Mountains appears, one of the most breathtaking of many such views this area has to offer. As you continue northwest, several spur roads lead to ranch cabins in the valley, and a free-form fenceline of undulating logs (if it's visible above the snowline) defines the west side of the road as it continues through meadows with borders of aspen. You're now skiing along the Rio Chama, in its passage down from the Continental Divide in the San Juan peaks.

At about 6 miles you cross into the Rio Grande National Forest (designated by a sign), where a spur road goes down to the left into a campground by the river. There is a complex of corrals by the river, too, along with an old trailer, summer headquarters for the cowboys who tend the cattle grazing the valley meadows. This is one of my favorite places on earth; we come here in the summertime to camp and fish and climb the 9-mile trail up the valley to the Continental Divide. In the wintertime there is even more peace and beauty afforded by the snow-covered river valley and the red and white peaks of the high country. This is about as far as you'll want to go for a day trip; the road continues past the campground and eventually dead ends high up on the north ridge of the valley.

Because the road is largely open and exposed, snow conditions vary according to snowfall and temperature. Ski this route after a fresh snow, but on a day when clear skies show you the views—*they* are the trip. Snowmobiles do use the area.

CHAMA COMMUNITY TRAIL: 12 miles
Class I-II   6.4 kilometers   Elevation: 10,000 feet

This ski touring area, located on the west side of the highway just before Cumbres Pass, is maintained by several ski groups, who offer lessons and a groomed loop track of 6.4 kilometers. This is also where the Chama Chile Ski Classic is held every February.

The loop heads northwest from the highway along the railroad track to the 1-kilometer mark where it turns south, then southeast. At the 2-kilometer mark you can return to the railroad tracks via a spur trail, or continue southeast along the rest of the route, which winds around through varied terrain back towards the highway and the trailhead. There is no track fee.

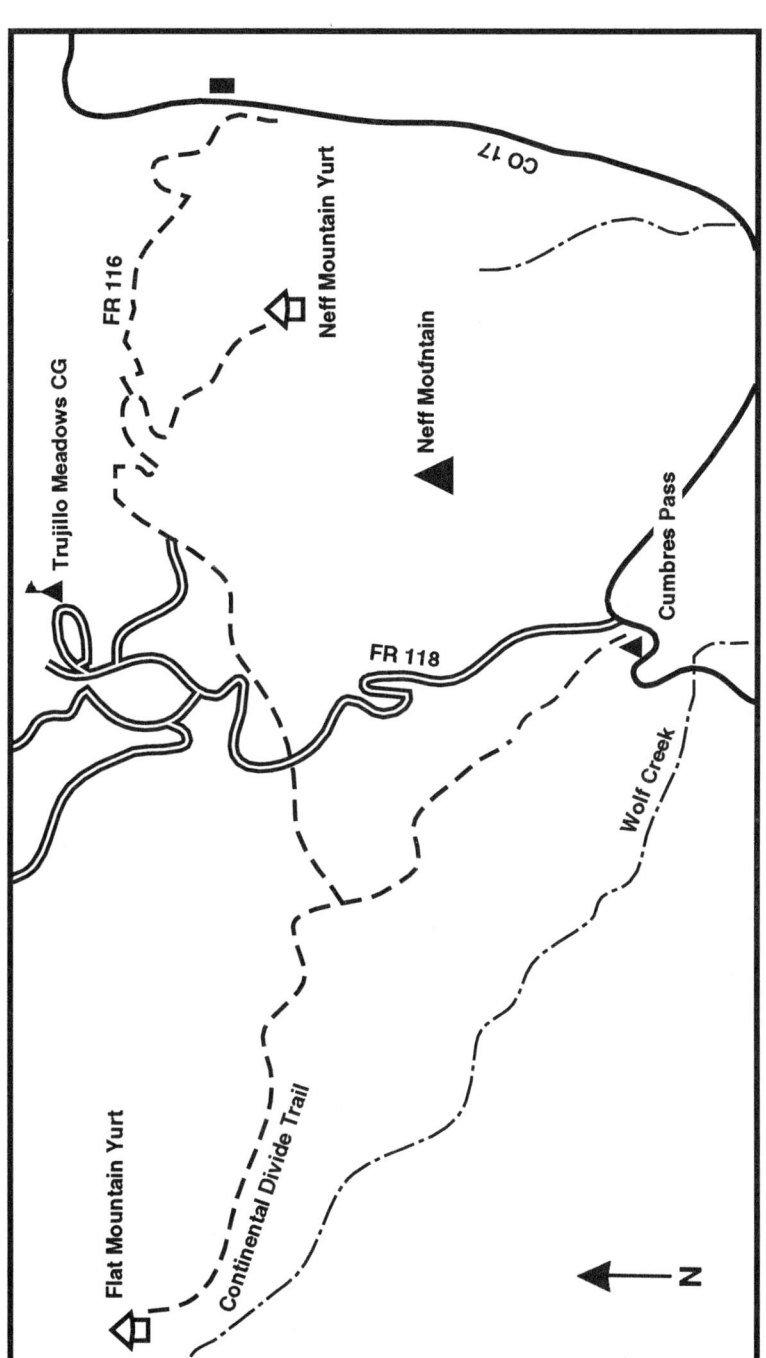

CUMBRES PASS AREA

TRUJILLO MEADOWS, FOREST ROAD 118: 13.9 miles
Class I-II   8 miles   Elevation: 10,000-10,400 feet

One of the most popular cross-country ski tours of the Cumbres Pass area, the forest road into Trujillo Reservoir offers moderate terrain amidst alpine scenery. The trailhead lies just beyond the top of Cumbres Pass—10,022 feet—and the Cumbres and Toltec Railroad junction house, where in the summertime the narrow-gauge scenic train stops en route to Antonito or Chama. There is room to park here, on the west side of the highway, or at the pass pull-out on the east side. The Continental Divide Trail, marked by a sign that may not be visible in the deep Colorado snow, (the orange blaze indicating the route to Flat Mountain Yurt is visible) leads northwest to Dipping Lakes—12 miles—and Blue Lake—22 miles—high up on the Continental Divide.

Trujillo Meadows Road travels northwest along the east side of the canyon. Rolling aspen meadows define the terrain along the

Backpacking on Cumbres Pass

first part of the moderate climb to the spruce-fir forest. We once came to ski the Chama area in February, in the midst of a snowstorm, and were unable to even distinguish the road in the 10-foot snowdrifts that covered these meadows. I found myself regretting that the snowmobilers, whom I usually try to avoid, had not yet been out to make a track through the thigh-deep snow so I could figure out where I was going. Normally, however, the route is well traveled and easy to follow.

Several switchbacks in the road climb to the denser forest canopy, and about $1^1/_2$ miles in the ascent levels out, then begins a moderate descent. A little farther on a sign indicates a turn to Spruce Park, 4 miles to the left, and Trujillo Reservoir 2 miles to the east (right). The route continues downhill to the next junction right to FR 116, leading to Neff Mountain, and soon after that a sign indicates another turn right to Trujillo Meadows Campground. You can take this turn for a shorter trip, ski to the campground and follow the loop roads through the campsite. The main road continues to the reservoir, with views of the high San Juan peaks to the west. A trail sign indicates Los Pinos Trail to the west, which follows the Rio de Los Pinos, and eventually connects to the Continental Divide Trail. The reservoir lies just east around the bend from the trail in a large meadow.

CONTINENTAL DIVIDE TRAIL #831 (to Flat Mountain Yurt): 13.9 miles

Class II   9 miles   Elevation: 10,000-11,100 feet

The Continental Divide Trail is also accessed from Cumbres Pass and leads all the way to the South San Juan Wilderness. A good day trip can take you the $4^1/_2$ miles to Flat Mountain Yurt, operated by Southwest Nordic Center out of Taos. Reservations must be made in advance to stay at the yurt. You can access the trail from the railroad sheds by skiing northwest to the orange blazes marking the trail, or park at the Trujillo Meadow trailhead and pick up the trail at the large orange circle (the route has been blazed by Southwest Nordic Center).

The trail starts out along FR 119, northwest across the meadow and up the ridge into the trees. Orange blazes hang from trees and mark the route. The trail follows the north side of the Wolf Creek drainage through rolling meadow terrain in a steady uphill climb. At about 2 miles is the junction with the trail east to Neff Mountain Yurt, marked with yellow blazes. About one-half mile beyond that junction the trail enters a large meadow, the halfway point to Flat Mountain Yurt. The trail crosses the meadow to the remains of an abandoned car sticking up through the snow, indicating the last of the road before the Divide Trail begins.

The trail continues into the trees, and the last mile is through steeper, more densely forested terrain. The yurt route actually leaves the Divide Trail and continues following the north ridge of Wolf Creek. An old burn area indicates that you are almost at the yurt site. The yurt itself sits in a protected pocket of trees just on the north side of the burn area, a site for sore eyes for those skiers with backpacks, ready to find shelter for the night.

The Continental Divide Trail continues northwest to the South San Juan Wilderness. North of the yurt you will find a huge bowl ideal for practicing telemark turns. Be aware of snow conditions and avalanche danger before exploring the terrain around the yurt. The ridge behind the Yurt affords views west to Flat Mountain and Banded Peak, north to the San Juans, northeast to the Trujillo Meadows area, and east to CO 17 at Cumbres Pass.

FOREST ROAD 116 (to Trujillo Meadows or Neff Mountain Yurt): 17.3 miles

Class I-II   6-8 miles   Elevation: 9,800-10,600 feet

Forest Road 116 can be skied as an alternate route to Trujillo Meadows or to Neff Mountain Yurt, also run by Southwest Nordic Center of Taos. The trailhead is north of Cumbres Pass, marked by the yellow water tank on the east side of the highway and the large, round blue sign indicating the forest road to the west.

Follow FR 116, or Neff Mountain Road, northwest up the hill until blue blazes (set up by Southwest Nordic Center) guide you

Flat Mountain Yurt

into the trees. The road travels 2 miles in a gradual climb to the junction with an old forest road which turns west (left) to Neff Mountain Yurt. Blue blazes continue to mark the route. Yellow blazes continue along FR 116 marking the route to Flat Mountain Yurt.

To find Neff Mountain Yurt, follow the blue blazes for about 1 mile through the trees until the trail enters a meadow area; the yurt sits across the meadow to the south, hidden from view. Continue along the road to the left of the clump of trees, then leave the road to follow the blazes to the yurt.

To continue to Trujillo Meadows, follow the yellow blazes west along FR 116 another 2 miles to the junction with Trujillo Meadows Reservoir Road (FR 118), which leads north to the campground. The yellow blazes continue west along an interconnecting route to Flat Mountain Trail.

YURT TO YURT TRAIL:
Class I-II 3½ miles Elevation: 10,200-10,400 feet

Southwest Nordic Center has marked a route that leads between its two yurts, Neff Mountain and Flat Mountain. To follow the route from Neff Mountain Yurt, follow the previous directions to FR 116. Instead of turning off FR 116 at the 2-mile mark to Neff Mountain, continue on FR 116 approximately 2 miles to the junction with FR 118, Trujillo Meadows Reservoir Road, which heads north to the campground and reservoir. Follow the yellow blazes west, across the road, and into the trees. The trail ascends to relatively flat meadow terrain before the junction with Flat Mountain Trail, blazed with orange diamonds. Turn northwest (right) along the trail to Flat Mountain Yurt or southeast (left) back to Cumbres Pass.

RED LAKE TRAIL, FOREST ROAD 114: 20.5 miles
Class I 6 miles Elevation: 10,200-10,600 feet

This easy forest road leads northwest to La Manga Creek and continues as a hiking trail to Red Lake at 11,500 feet. Beginner skiers can ski through the meadows, across the creek, and along the valley to where the trail ascends the canyon.

SPRUCE HOLE, FOREST ROAD 108: 21.2 miles
Class II 6 miles Elevation:10,200-10,600 feet

Forest Road 108 at the north end of the Pinorealosa Mountains leads northeast from the highway in a tour that affords views of the Conejos River Canyon, San Luis Valley, Sangre de Cristos, and Conejos Peak. The road leads northeast to a junction at the north end of the mountains; both roads lead southeast on either side of a meadow area to Spruce Hole.

BIBLIOGRAPHY

Baldwin, Edwin R. *Skiing Cross-country*. New York: McGraw Hill, 1977.

Beard, Sam. *Ski Touring in Northern New Mexico*. Albuquerque: Nordic Press, 1991.

Burns, Jim, and Cheryl Lemanski. *Skiing the Sun—Ski Touring in New Mexico's National Forests*. Los Alamos: Los Alamos Ski Touring, 1983.

Caldwell, John. *The New Cross-Country Ski Book*. Brattleboro, Vermont: The Stephen Greene Press.

Crawford-Currie, Ronald. *Cross-country Skiing*. New York: Van Nostrand Reinhold, 1982.

Gillette, Ned, and John Dostal. *Cross-country Skiing*. Bantam Books, 1984.

Liebers, Arthur. *The Complete Book of Cross-country Skiing and Ski Touring*. New York: Coward, McCann and Geoghegan, 1974.

Matthews, Kay. *Hiking Trails of the Sandia and Manzano Mountains*. El Valle, New Mexico: Acequia Madre Press, 1991.

Matthews, Kay. *Hiking the Wilderness—A Backpacking Guide to the Wheeler Peak, Pecos, and San Pedro Parks Wilderness Areas*. El Valle, New Mexico: Acequia Madre Press, 1992.

Overhage, Carl. *Six One-Day Walks in the Pecos Wilderness*. Santa Fe: Sunstone Press, 1984.

Santa Fe Group of the Sierra Club. *Day Hikes in the Santa Fe Area*.

Santa Fe: National Education Association Press, 1981.

Shields, Brian, and Richard Erickson. *Ski Touring Trails—Taos, Angel Fire, Red River.* Taos: Taos Mountain Outfitters, 1978.

Tejada-Flores, Lito. *Back-country Skiing: The Sierra Club Guide to Skiing Off the Beaten Track.* San Francisco: Sierra Club Books, 1981.

Tinker, Gene. *Let's Learn Ski Touring: Your Guide to Cross-Country Fun.* New York: Walker and Company, 1971.

Ungnade, Herbert. *Guide to New Mexico Mountains.* Albuquerque: University of New Mexico Press, 1965.

Wiik, Sven, and David Summer. *The Regnery Guide to Ski Touring.* Chicago: Henry Regnery Company, 1974.

GLOSSARY

AVALANCHE: Heavy snowfall on mountain slopes where the steep terrain is unable to hold the snow in place.

BASE WAX: Undercoat of hot wax applied to fiberglass skis at the beginning of the season. Also referred to as glider wax.

BIVOUAC: Emergency camp made in the snow with improvised shelter.

CABLE BINDING: Binding which secures the heel of the boot on the ski for use in back-country skiing.

CAMBER: A ski's stiffness or flexibility when it contacts the snow under your weight. Also referred to as purchase.

DIAGONAL STRIDE: Basic forward motion used in cross-country skiing.

DOUBLE-POLING: Using both poles simultaneously to pull-push across the snow in a glide.

DUOFOLD: Double layer cotton-wool long underwear.

FALL LINE: The path of least resistance on a hill.

FROSTBITE: Exposure of extremities to severe cold resulting in damaged nerves and tissue.

GAITERS: Protective leggings worn on the lower leg, made of waterproof material.

GLIDER WAX: Undercoat of hot wax applied to fiberglass skis at the beginning of the season. Also referred to as base wax.

GRIP WAX: Applied over base wax to correspond to temperature and snow condition, to provide both glide and grip. Available in a wide array of color-coded tins.

HARD WAX: A grip that corresponds to cold, new snow conditions.

HERRINGBONE: Uphill ski technique that employs a wide V and friction of inside ski edges for grip.

KICKER ZONE: The area of the ski that comes in direct contact with the snow under your body weight. Usually measures a foot or so in front of and behind your foot.

KICK TURN: A technique to negotiate a 180° turn in a stationary position.

KLISTER: A sticky grip wax used when the snow has melted and refrozen.

MOGUL: Small bump of hard snow on downhill ski slopes.

PINE TAR: Sticky coating used as undercoat preparation on wooden skis at the beginning of the season.

POLYPROPYLENE: Plastic, nonabsorbent material used in the manufacture of ski clothing.

PURCHASE: A ski's stiffness or flexibility when it contacts the snow under your weight. Also referred to as camber.

RIPARIAN: The environment contiguous to a river or stream.

SKATING: A skiing technique that employs a side-to-side gliding motion like that of ice skating.

SNOWPLOW: A downhill technique that uses a wedge and inside edging to slow speed or stop.

SNOW SEAL: Waterproof coating applied to ski boots.

SOFT WAX: A grip wax that corresponds to old, melted snow.

SPACE BLANKET: An insulating, fireproof cover that can be used for protection against cold and heat.

STEM CHRISTIE: A downhill technique that is a cross between a snowplow turn and the parallel turn used in alpine skiing.

TELEMARK: A downhill technique used on steep or powder slopes.

TOE BINDING: The most common cross-country binding that secures the front of the boot and leaves the heel free for uphill technique.

TRAVERSE: An uphill technique that resembles a zig-zag climb up a hill across an open slope.

WAXABLE: Skis that require an application of grip waxes.

WAXLESS: Machine-bottomed skis that require no application of grip wax.